BASIC YIDDISH: A GI AND WORKBOOK

Basic Yiddish: A Grammar and Workbook comprises an accessible reference grammar with related exercises in a single volume.

The workbook is structured around 25 short units, each presenting relevant grammar points which are explained using multiple examples in jargon-free language.

Basic Yiddish is suitable for both class use as well as independent study. Key features include:

- a clear, accessible format
- many useful language examples
- jargon-free explanations of grammar
- abundant exercises with a full answer key

Clearly presented and user-friendly, *Basic Yiddish* provides readers with the essential tools to express themselves in a wide variety of situations, making it an ideal grammar reference and practice resource for both beginners and students with some knowledge of the language.

Rebecca Margolis is Associate Professor at the University of Ottawa, Canada.

Other titles available in the Grammar Workbooks series are:

Basic Cantonese
Intermediate Cantonese

Basic Chinese
Intermediate Chinese

Basic German
Intermediate German

Basic Italian

Basic Irish
Intermediate Irish

Basic Japanese
Intermediate Japanese

Basic Korean
Intermediate Korean

Basic Polish
Intermediate Polish

Basic Russian
Intermediate Russian

Basic Spanish
Intermediate Spanish

Basic Welsh
Intermediate Welsh

BASIC YIDDISH: A GRAMMAR AND WORKBOOK

Rebecca Margolis

LONDON AND NEW YORK

First published 2011
by Routledge
2 Park Square, Milton Park, Abingdon, Oxon OX14 4RN

Simultaneously published in the USA and Canada
by Routledge
711 Third Avenue, New York, NY 10017

Routledge is an imprint of the Taylor & Francis Group, an informa business

British Library Cataloguing in Publication Data
A catalogue record for this book is available from the British Library

Library of Congress Cataloging in Publication Data
A catalog record for this book has been requested

ISBN: 978-0-415-55521-0 (hbk)
ISBN: 978-0-415-55522-7 (pbk)
ISBN: 978-0-203-80887-0 (ebk)

Typeset in Times Ten and New Peninim MT
by Graphicraft Limited, Hong Kong

Printed and bound in Great Britain by
CPI Antony Rowe, Chippenham, Wiltshire

CONTENTS

PREFACE

This text offers a basic introduction to Standard Yiddish (*klal-yidish*) grammar along with practice exercises. Its aim is to provide an accessible survey of Yiddish grammatical structures for the beginner as well as the more advanced Yiddish learner. It assumes previous familiarity with the Yiddish alphabet and the ability to read printed Yiddish. This book is intended to supplement other textbooks and learning materials and/or serve as grammar reference and practice for all speakers of Yiddish. Each unit contains an overview of grammatical forms with explanations and tables as well as examples. Note: Tables are read from right to left. It introduces a small working vocabulary for the purposes of examples and practice in exercises, with Yiddish vocabulary words listed in alphabetical order in the glossary at the back. Chapters conclude with exercises designed to allow learners to practice using the new grammatical form: form identification, matching, fill-in-the-blank, manipulation of a grammatical form, translation into English, translation into Yiddish, and so on. A full answer key to all exercises is provided at the end of the text.

Preliminary notes

1. Terminology

Yiddish is an *inflected* language. That is, words change forms to express grammatical categories of nouns (gender, number, case) as well as verbal forms (person, tense, mood, and aspect). *Conjugation* refers to the inflection of verbs; *declension* refers to the inflection of nouns, adjectives and pronouns. *Stress* refers to which syllable of a word receives the emphasis. In Yiddish, most words have penultimate stress: the second-to-last syllable is stressed.

Example: mother ***mame*** **מאַמע**. Suffixes on words do not count as syllables.

2. Yiddish variation

There is variation in Yiddish due to the language's many dialects. Further, there is no universally agreed-upon set of rules regarding Yiddish orthography.

The system employed in this text is the most commonly taught and published form of the language in academic and secular contexts: Standard Yiddish (*klal-yidish*), devised by the YIVO Institute for Jewish Research. However, today the majority of Yiddish publications are produced in religious communities which use a variety of spelling systems.

3. Loshn-koydesh *לשון-קודש*

Loshn-koydesh refers to the pre-Modern Hebrew-Aramaic component of Yiddish, which constitutes elements that stem from Biblical, Talmudic and other rabbinic texts. These words are fully integrated into Yiddish (the way that elements of Greek origin are integrated into English), but, unlike the rest of Standard Yiddish, they are not spelled phonetically. That is, they are not spelled the way they are pronounced.

Example: wedding (pronounced *khasene*) חתונה.

The proportion of *loshn-koydesh* words in Yiddish ranges from text to text. For the sake of reading ease, this text uses a minimal number of words of *loshn-koydesh* derivation in the vocabulary lists and examples.

Selected bibliography of books for reference and further study

Grammar textbooks

Estraikh, Gennady, *Intensive Yiddish* (Oxford: Oksforder Yidish Press, 1996).

Schaechter, Mordkhe, *Yiddish II: An Intermediate and Advanced Textbook* (New York: League for Yiddish, 1986, 1993, 1995, 2003).

Weinreich, Uriel, *College Yiddish: An Introduction to the Yiddish Language and to Jewish Life and Culture* (New York: YIVO Institute for Jewish Research, 1949). Several subsequent editions.

Zucker, Sheva, *Yiddish: An Introduction to the Language, Literature and Culture*, Volume 1 (Hoboken, NJ: KTAV Publishing House, 1994).

——, *Yiddish: An Introduction to the Language, Literature and Culture*, Volume 2 (New York: Workmen's Circle, 2002).

Yiddish reference grammars

Birnbaum, Salomo A., *Yiddish: A Survey and a Grammar* (Toronto: University of Toronto Press, 1979).

Jacobs, Neil G., *Yiddish: A Linguistic Introduction* (Cambridge, UK: Cambridge University Press, 2005).

Katz, Dovid, *Grammar of the Yiddish Language* (London, UK: Gerald Duckworth & Co Ltd, 1987).

Mark, Yudl, *Gramatik fun der yidisher klal-shprakh* [Grammar of Standard Yiddish] (New York: Congress for Jewish Culture, 1978).

Schaechter, Mordkhe, *Takones fun yidishn oysleyg* [The Standardized Yiddish Orthography]; *Fun folkshprakh tsu kultursprakh* [The History of the Standardized Yiddish Spelling] (New York: League for Yiddish, YIVO Institute for Jewish Research, 1999).

Zaretski, Ayzik, *Praktishe yidishe gramatik* [Practical Yiddish Grammar] (Moscow: Farlag "shul un bukh", 1926, 1927, 1929).

Dictionaries

Harkavy, Alexander. *Yiddish-English-Hebrew Dictionary* (New York: Hebrew Publishing Company, 1910). Numerous subsequent editions.

Joffe, Yudah A., and Yudl Mark, eds. *Groyser ẏerṭerbukh fun der yidisher shprakh*, 4 volumes (New York: Ḳomiṭeṭ farn groysn ẏerṭerbukh fun der yidisher shprakh, 1961–1980). Only the letter *alef* has been published.

Niborski, Yitskhak. *Verterbukh fun loshn-koydesh-shtamike verter/ Dictionnaire des mots d'origine hébraïque et araméenne en usage dans la langue yiddish* (Paris: Medem Bibliotek, 1997).

Kerner, Samuel and Bernard Vaisbrot. *Frantseyzish/yidish-verterbukh/ Dictionnaire Français-Yiddish* (Paris: Bibliothèque Medem, 2000).

Niborski, Yitskhok and Bernard Vaisbrot. *Yidish-frantseyzish verterbukh/ Dictionnaire Yiddish-Français* (Paris: Bibliothèque Medem, 2002).

Weinreich, Uriel. *English-Yiddish/Yiddish-English Dictionary* (New York: YIVO Institute for Jewish Research, Schocken Books, 1968). Several subsequent editions.

UNIT 1

Introduction to nouns, articles, attributive adjectives, noun phrases, the nominative case, pronouns

Nouns

A noun is a part of speech that refers to a person, other living thing, object, place or abstract idea. Examples of nouns include: mother, class, city, and greatness.

All Yiddish nouns possess three characteristics known as (1) *gender*, (2) *number*, and (3) *case.*

1. Gender

Gender refers to three fixed grammatical categories into which all nouns fall: masculine, feminine, and neuter. In Yiddish, the Yiddish word for every noun has a fixed gender: e.g. "man" is masculine in gender, as is "class." All nouns belong to one of these three grammatical categories, including all animate, inanimate objects and abstract concepts. Gender must be learned with each noun.

A word of caution regarding the concept of "gender"

As a rule, nouns that are semantically masculine (i.e. they refer to nouns that are biologically male) are masculine in gender (e.g. brother, father), and semantically female nouns are female (e.g. sister, mother). Small things are often neuter (e.g. baby, puppy).

However, gender in Yiddish functions simply as a way of categorizing nouns into grammatical categories: a class or a park is not "male" because it is masculine; masculine simply tells us what the forms of the definite article ("the") and adjective (example: good) that form a noun phrase with "class" or "park" will take. In Yiddish, the words "the" and "good" in the phrases "the good class" or "the good park" will have the same form as "the good person" (also masculine) but different forms from the noun phrases "the good mother" or "the good city" (both feminine) or "the good book" (neuter). There is no reliable, universal way for most nouns to tell whether they will be masculine, feminine or neuter.

In sum, masculine gender does not refer to "maleness" and feminine gender does not refer to "femaleness." Rather, gender is one of three grammatical categories that determine the form a given noun phrase (definite article and/or adjective + noun) will take in a Yiddish sentence.

Vocabulary: examples of nouns and their genders

Translation	Example of noun	Gender
person, human being	מענטש	masculine
mother	מאַמע	feminine
book	בוך	neuter

Note the differences in the form of the word "the" and the endings on the adjective "good" in these examples:

the good person — **דער גוטער מענטש**
the good mother — **די גוטע מאַמע**
the good book — **דאָס גוטע בוך**

Yiddish compound nouns (nouns made up of a noun fused to another noun/an adjective/a verbal base), take on the gender of the second noun.

Example:

the homework — די היימאַרבעט

2. Number

Number refers to singular (one) or plural (more than one). Yiddish nouns as well as their definite articles and adjectives inflect in the plural.

Yiddish has several ways of forming plurals. These can include endings such as ס or ן, changes in the word itself, and other variations. These do not necessarily correspond to the form of the singular or the gender of the noun and should be learned.

Examples of nouns and their plural forms:

Translation	Plural form of noun	Singular form of noun
people	מענטשן	מענטש
mothers	מאַמעס	מאַמע
books	ביכער	בוך

3. Case

The case of a noun indicates its grammatical function relative to the verb: Is it doing the action? Is it receiving the action? Is it next to/under/about something? Cases embody a system of inflection to indicate these functions. Yiddish has three cases: *nominative*, *accusative*, and *dative*. The nominative case will be discussed more fully later in this unit; the accusative and dative cases will be presented in separate units.

Cases are also called "*declensions*." When the forms of definite articles ("the"), adjectives, and personal pronouns change forms according to gender, number and case, this is called *declining*.

Articles

Yiddish articles appear in two forms: indefinite and definite.

1. The indefinite article ("a")

The indefinite article ("a") refers to a generic, non-specific noun or nouns (a person or people). It means "any" member of the category of this noun. In the singular it always appears as אַ or אַן (the form of אַ before a vowel): it is never inflected (does not change form according to gender and case).

The plural indefinite is formed without an article, as in English: e.g. *a* person (singular); people (plural). It is not inflected.

Examples in the singular form:

Translation	Definite article-noun phrase	Indefinite article "a"
a (any) person	אַ מענטש	
a (any) mother	אַ מאַמע	אַ
a (any) book	אַ בוך	

Examples in the plural form:

Translation	Indefinite article-noun phrase	Indefinite article "a"
(any) people	מענטשן	
(any) mothers	מאַמעס	*none*
(any) books	ביכער	

2. The definite article "the"

The definite article "the" refers to a specific noun or nouns (the person, this person, the people, these people). Definite articles decline: their forms are determined by the gender, number and case of the noun.

As discussed in Unit 24, the Yiddish definite article can also function as demonstrative adjectives with the meaning of an implicit "this".

Examples in the singular form:

Translation	Definite article-noun phrase	Definite article "the"
the (specific) person	דער מענטש	דער
the (specific) mother	די מאַמע	די
the (specific) book	דאָס בוך	דאָס

Examples in the plural form:

Translation	Definite article-noun phrase	Definite article "the"
the (specific) people	די מענטשן	
the (specific) mothers	די מאַמעס	די
the (specific) books	די ביכער	

Attributive adjectives

An adjective is a part of speech that describes a noun, such as "good" or "small." In Yiddish, the shortest form of an adjective is called the base form.

Vocabulary: examples of adjectives

Translation	Adjective
good	גוט
great, large	גרויס
happy	פֿריילעך
small	קליין
nice, attractive	שיין

An adjective that describes a noun is known as an *attributive* (*descriptive*) adjective. Its position follows the article and precedes the noun it modifies. In its form, it shares the same gender, number and case as the noun, and inflects accordingly. Inflection is indicated by special endings on the base forms of the adjectives.

Attributive adjective base endings

This chart offers a comparison of the masculine, feminine and neuter definite singular forms as well as the plural form in the nominative case (see below). A sample noun is provided as an example of each.

Translation	Examples: adjective-noun	Example: adjective base form	Ending on adjective base	Gender
good person	גוטער מענטש		־ער	masculine
good mother	גוטע מאַמע		־ע	feminine
good book	גוטע בוך	גוט	־ע	neuter
good people good mothers good books	גוטע מענטשן גוטע מאַמעס גוטע ביכער		־ע	plural (all genders)

Noun phrases

Nouns often appear in *noun phrases* together with an *article* (“a” or “the”) and an *attributive adjective*.

In a Yiddish noun phrase, the article, adjective and noun must always "agree" (match) in gender, number and case. That is, if a noun is masculine in gender, singular in number, and nominative in case, its article and adjective must appear in the corresponding forms.

The forms for articles and adjectives follow set patterns that will be presented in this text, with the forms for the word "the" and the endings on the adjective changing depending on the gender, number and case of the noun they are modifying.

Important things to note:

1. Adjectives decline (take adjective endings) only when they precede a noun in a noun phrase.
2. With a very few exceptions, nouns only decline in the plural.

The nominative case

The nominative case refers to the noun (and its article/adjective), that is the "doer" of the verb.

For example: "The nice child reads a book under the green tree."

Who is the "doer" of the verb, i.e. who is doing the action of reading? The child.

In the above sample sentence, the Yiddish noun phrase "The nice child" is in the nominative case, with the article and adjective agreeing with "child."

Nominative case

Translation	Sample noun phrase	Attributive adjective ending on base	Article	Sample noun	Gender number
the good person	דער גוטער מענטש	ער–	definite דער	מענטש	masculine singular
a good person	אַ גוטער מענטש	ער–	indefinite אַ		
the good mother	די גוטע מאַמע	ע–	definite די	מאַמע	feminine singular
a good mother	אַ גוטע מאַמע	ע–	indefinite אַ		
the good book	דאָס גוטע בוך	ע–	the דאָס	בוך	neuter singular
a good book	אַ גוט בוך	*no ending*	indefinite אַ		

Translation	Sample noun phrase	Attributive adjective ending on base	Article	Sample noun	Gender number
the good people the good mothers the good books	די גוטע מענטשן די גוטע מאַמעס די גוטע ביכער	–ע	the די	מענטשן מאַמעס ביכער	plural all genders
good people good mothers good books	גוטע מענטשן גוטע מאַמעס גוטע ביכער	–ע	indefinite –		

The noun phrase "די גוט מענטש" is grammatically incorrect in Yiddish, because the forms of the article and adjective do not agree with the noun in gender, number and case. Because the word מענטש is masculine and singular, the correct form of the phrase in the nominative case is "דער גוטער מענטש".

Note: Yiddish noun phrases in the neuter indefinite as well as all plural forms retain the same endings in all cases.

Notes on article-adjective-noun agreement:

If an indefinite article אַ or אַן refers to masculine, feminine or plural nouns, the adjective takes the same form as it would with the definite article. This is true in all cases.

דער גוטער מענטש – אַ גוטער מענטש
די גוטע מאַמע – אַ גוטע מאַמע
די גוטע ביכער – גוטע ביכער

However, if an indefinite article refers to a neuter noun, then its adjective remains in its base form. This is true for all cases.

דאָס גוטע בוך – אַ גוט בוך

Pronouns

Pronouns stand in for nouns. In Yiddish, pronouns change their form to indicate number, gender, and case as well as *person*: first person (I, we), second person (you) or third person (he, she, it, one, they). There are a few pronouns that never decline, such as *what* וואָס.

A personal pronoun replaces a specific person or thing. A personal pronoun will share the same person, number, gender and case as the noun it is replacing.

For example: *The mother* is sleeping. = *She* is sleeping.

Here are the pronouns in the nominative case, which indicates that the personal pronoun is "the doer" the verb (i.e. is the subject of the verb; for example, I write).

Personal pronouns in the nominative case

Personal pronoun	Person, number, translation
איך	First person singular: I
דו	Second person singular: you/thou The familiar, informal form akin to *tu* in French
ער	Third person singular masculine: he
זי	Third person singular feminine: she
עס (also סע/ ס')	Third person singular neuter: it Can also function as a placeholder in a sentence without a logical subject Example: It is raining עס גייט אַ רעגן
מען (also מע/ מ')	Third person singular impersonal: one (they) A way of forming the passive in Yiddish: Example: One knows, it is known מען ווייס
מיר	First person plural: we
איר	Second person plural: you Also used for the formal form akin to *vous* in French
זיי	Third person plural: they

Exercise 1.1

For each noun on the list below, identify the gender, number and case. When in doubt, check the vocabulary list above. Note: All nouns in this unit's exercises are nominative.

Example:

gender: feminine; number: singular; case: nominative   *מאַמע*

1. בוך
2. מענטשן
3. מאַמעס
4. ביכער
5. מענטש

Exercise 1.2

Write in the correct matching form of the definite ("the") and indefinite ("a") article and adjective. Refer to exercise 1 above and the nominative case chart.

Example:

ד_______ גוט_______ מענטש \ _______ גוט_______ מענטש

מענטש masculine, singular, nominative

דער גוטער מענטש \ אַ גוטער מענטש

1. ד_______ גוט_______ בוך \ _______ גוט_______ בוך
2. ד_______ גוט_______ ביכער \ _______ גוט_______ ביכער
3. ד_______ גוט_______ מאַמע \ _______ גוט_______ מאַמע
4. ד_______ גוט_______ מאַמעס \ _______ גוט_______ מאַמעס
5. ד_______ גוט_______ מענטשן \ _______ גוט_______ מענטשן

Exercise 1.3

Replace each noun or noun phrase with the corresponding pronoun.

Note: The pronoun should match the original noun in gender, number, and case.

If the noun is:	The pronoun to replace it is:
masculine singular	ער
feminine singular	זי
neuter singular	עס
all plurals	זיי

Example:

אַ קלײנער מענטש *masculine, singular, nominative*
ער *The pronoun is also third person, masculine, singular, nominative*

1. די מאַמעס
2. דאָס גרויסע בוך
3. שײנע מענטשן
4. די ביכער
5. אַ פֿרײלעכע מאַמע

Exercise 1.4

Translate the following noun phrases into English.

1. די קלײנע ביכער
2. אַ פֿרײלעכער מענטש
3. גוטע מאַמעס
4. די שײנע ביכער
5. די גרויסע מאַמע

Exercise 1.5

Translate the following noun phrases into Yiddish.

1. This great book
2. A small book
3. The good mother
4. A nice/attractive person
5. Happy people

UNIT 2

Introduction to verbs, regular verbs in the present indicative tense

Introduction to verbs

A verb is a word that expresses an action or a state of being.

For example: to run, to dance, to be, to remember.

The infinitive form of a Yiddish verb ends in either ן– or ען–.

There are three primary qualities that Yiddish verbs can express:

1. Tense: provides information about *when in time* an action is taking place: now (present tense); in the past and not now (past tense); in the future and not now (future tense).
2. Mood: provides information about the modality of an action. It can include actions that take place in time (the indicative) or an action that is not actually taking place but is commanded (imperative mood), desired/hypothetical (subjunctive), or contingent upon other factors (conditional).
3. Aspect: provides information about the way that the action is taking place: its duration, frequency, and so on. This category includes such markers as prefixes on verbs.

Conjugation

Yiddish verbs conjugate, with the form of the verb matching its doer and reflecting when or how the verb is taking place.

All verbs contain an inflected part where different endings are added onto the base form (infinitive minus the ן– or ען– ending). Some verbs can take additional parts: for example, for the past and future tenses, Yiddish verbs contain a past participle and infinitive, respectively.

Regular verbs in the present indicative tense

The present indicative tense refers to the time that the utterance is being made. It is also used in general statements that do not contain a specific reference to time and for actions that are ongoing/uncompleted. The Yiddish present indicative form corresponds to any of the following English constructions: I eat. I do eat. I am eating. I have been eating.

Yiddish verbs fall into the categories of regular and irregular verbs. Regular verbs conform to the standard conjugation pattern outlined in the chart below. They are predictable. Irregular verbs do not conform to the standard conjugation pattern in some way. These will be presented in separate units.

Vocabulary: examples of regular verbs

Translation	Base of verb *infinitive minus* ן / ען	Infinitive of verb
to become	ווער	ווערן
to read	לייען	לייענען
to eat	עס	עסן
to sleep	שלאָפֿ	שלאָפֿן
to write	שרײַב	שרײַבן

How to form the present indicative of Yiddish verbs

1. Determine the base of the verb: infinitive (dictionary form) minus the ן / ען ending
2. Add the appropriate endings for each person to the base.

Present indicative tense conjugation

Example 2 לייענען base = לייען	Example 1 שלאָפֿן base = שלאָפֿ	Ending on verb base	Person, personal pronoun
איך לייען	איך שלאָף	*no ending*	First person singular: I
דו לייענסט	דו שלאָפֿסט	סט–	Second person singular: you
ער לייענט	ער שלאָפֿט	ט–	Third person singular masculine: he
זי לייענט	זי שלאָפֿט	ט–	Third person singular feminine: she
עס לייענט	עס שלאָפֿט	ט–	Third person singular neuter: it

Example 2 לייענען base = לייענ	Example 1 שלאָפֿן base = שלאָפֿ	Ending on verb base	Person, personal pronoun
מען לייענט	מען שלאָפֿט	–ט	Third person singular impersonal: one
מיר לייענען	מיר שלאָפֿן	–ן/ –ען	First person plural: we
איר לייענט	איר שלאָפֿט	–ט	Second person plural: you
זיי לייענען	זיי שלאָפֿן	–ן/ –ען	Third person plural: they

Notes on the spelling of Yiddish verbs

Stems ending in ל, נ, מ, נג, נק after a consonant or a stressed vowel tend to end in ען in the infinitive. They conjugate with an ending of ען in the first and third person plural, even if they do not end in ען in the infinitive.

For example: the verb *to go* גיין (presented in Unit 10) is conjugated מיר/זיי גייען.

As a general rule, Yiddish does not double consonants. Thus, "you eat" in Yiddish is rendered דו עסט and not דו עססט.

Exercise 2.1

Provide the full conjugation in the present indicative of all the verbs in the vocabulary.

Example:

שרײַבן   איך שרײַב, דו...

1. ווערן
2. עסן
3. לייענען
4. שלאָפֿן

Exercise 2.2

Provide the correct present indicative ending for each of the verb forms below. The verbs have been provided in their base forms; simply add the appropriate endings.

Note: Make sure that each verb form matches its subject in person (first, second or third) and number (singular or plural).

Example:

זי שרײַב______
זי שרײַבט *third person singular*

1. איך ווער______
2. זי שלאָפֿ______
3. מיר עס______
4. איך לייענ______
5. זיי ווער______
6. מען שרײַב______
7. דו ווער______
8. ער לייענ______

Exercise 2.3

In each of the following sentences, locate the verb and identify its person (first, second or third) and its number (singular or plural).

Note: For verb conjugation, gender is not a relevant category as all third person verbs take the same form regardless of the gender of their subjects.

Example:

די פֿרוי לייענט. *person: third person; number: singular*

1. מיר עסן.
2. די מענטשן שרײַבן.
3. עס ווערט גרויס.
4. מען לייענט.
5. איך שלאָף.

Exercise 2.4

Translate each sentence in 2.3 into English.

Example:

די פֿרוי לייענט. *The woman reads/is reading.*

Exercise 2.5

Translate the following sentences into Yiddish.

1. The big person is reading.
2. They are becoming happy.
3. The small mother eats.
4. We read.
5. A nice book is read. One is reading a nice book.

UNIT 3

Irregular verb *to be* זײַן, the predicative (predicate nouns, pronouns and adjectives)

The irregular verb *to be* זײַן

Most Yiddish verbs follow a regular pattern of endings added onto a base that is formed from the infinitive form.

There are a number of Yiddish verbs that deviate from this pattern, known as irregular verbs. One of these irregular verbs is the verb "to be."

Note that, in this irregular verb, the base of the verb changes three times and that it does not take the expected verbal endings for the present indicative tense conjugation.

Conjugation of the verb זײַן in the present indicative tense

Translation	Conjugated form	Person, number
I am	איך בין	First person singular
You are	דו ביסט	Second person singular
He/she/it/one is	ער/זי/עס/מען איז	Third person singular
We are	מיר זײַנען	First person plural
You are	איר זײַט	Second person plural
They are	זיי זײַנען	Third person plural

Note: In Yiddish, the verb זײַן (along with the verb *to have* האָבן) is essential to forming the past tense, where it acts as the auxiliary (helping verb) along with a past participle form.

Example:

I *was/was being* a person. *איך בין געווען אַ מענטש.*

The predicative

The predicate in grammar refers to (1) the verb and (2) the subject of the verb and anything modifying (giving more information about) the subject of the verb.

Examples of predicates:

1. The good woman is reading.
2. She is a good woman.
3. The woman is good.

A predicative can be a noun or pronoun ("the good woman" in example 1 above, "she" and "a good woman" in example 2) or an adjective ("good" in example 3).

In examples 2 and 3, the linking verb is "is," and the complements after the linking verb are "a good woman" and "good" respectively. When the complement after a linking verb is a noun or pronoun, it is termed a predicate nominative (example 2). When the complement after a linking verb is an adjective, it is termed a predicate adjective (example 3).

זײַן is among a short list of verbs that act as linking verbs for predicate nominatives.

Examples:

I am **a mother**. **איך בין אַ מאַמע.**
It is **the book**. **עס איז דאָס בוך.**

Other verbs on this list include *to become* ווערן and *to remain* בלײַבן.

Note: In these cases, the predicate nominative is equivalent to the subject of the verb. Thus, in the first sentence, "I" is the same person as "a mother." Both are in the nominative case.

There are two forms of predicate adjectives in Yiddish.

1. A predicative adjective can appear in its base (dictionary) form, without an ending. It never inflects.

Examples:

The person is great. דער מענטש איז גרויס.
The mother is great. די מאַמע איז גרויס.
The book is great. דאָס בוך איז גרויס.
The people are becoming great. די מענטשן ווערן גרויס.

In all of the above cases, the predicative adjective “great”, גרויס is connected by the linking verbs *is* איז, or *becomes* ווערט to the subject nouns (person, mother, book, people).

2. A predicate adjective can inflect to agree with the subject in gender, number, and case if it is preceded by an article. In this case, it declines according to the regular endings in the masculine and feminine singular and all plural forms. Exception: the indefinite neuter predicate adjective has an ending of “ס.”

Examples:

The person is a good one.	דער מענטש איז **אַ** גוטער.
The person is the good one.	דער מענטש איז **דער** גוטער.
The mother is a good one.	די מאַמע איז **אַ** גוטע.
The mother is the good one.	די מאַמע איז **די** גוטע.
The book is a good one.	דאָס בוך איז **אַ** גוטס.
The book is the good one.	דאָס בוך איז **דאָס** גוטע.
The people are becoming good ones.	די מענטשן ווערן גוטע.
The people are becoming the good ones.	די מענטשן ווערן **די** גוטע.

Predicate adjectives can act as nouns when a person or thing is defined by an adjectival characteristic. In this case, the adjective declines according to gender, number and case.

Examples:

The good one (i.e. man) eats/is eating.	דער גוטער עסט.
The good one (i.e. woman) eats/is eating.	די גוטע שלאָפֿט.

Exercise 3.1

Provide the correct present indicative form of the verb זײַן in each sentence. Note: Make sure that each verb form matches its subject in person (first, second or third) and number (singular or plural).

Example:

third person singular = ער   *דער מענטש איז גרויס.*

1. מיר _______ גרויס.
2. די מאַמע _______ גרויס.
3. איך _______ גרויס.
4. אַלע ביכער _______ גרויס.
5. דו _______ גרויס.
6. איר _______ גרויס.
7. עס _______ גרויס.
8. מען _______ גרויס.
9. ער _______ גרויס.
10. זיי _______ גרויס.

Exercise 3.2

In each of the following sentences, identify:

a. verbs: identify tense, person and number.
b. subject noun/pronoun: identify gender and number (all are in the nominative case) for articles, attributive adjectives and nouns.
c. predicate nouns and adjectives: identify gender and number (all are in the nominative case).

Example:

דער גוטער מענטש איז פֿריילעך.

a. verb: איז present indicative tense, third person, singular
b. noun phrase: דער גוטער מענטש masculine, singular, nominative.
c. predicate adjective: פֿריילעך

1. איך ווער אַ פֿריילעכער מענטש.
2. זיי זײַנען גוטע ביכער.
3. דער מענטש איז אַ שיינער.
4. גוטע מענטשן זײַנען פֿריילעך.
5. דאָס בוך ווערט גוט.

Exercise 3.3

Translate the sentences in 3.2 into English.

Exercise 3.4

Translate the sentences into Yiddish.

1. I am great!
2. The little [one] (i.e. boy) is happy.
3. She is a good person.
4. That book is a small one.
5. The mother is small.

UNIT 4

Adverbs and adjective quantifiers

Adverbs

An adverb is a part of speech that can modify a verb, adjective or another adverb. It serves to answer questions such as when, where, how (in what way), and how much. In English, adverbs are often identifiable by their "-ly" ending (examples: quickly, happily, completely).

In Yiddish, uninflected adjectives serve as adverbs. There are other forms of adverbs that do not stem from adjectives, like the English "very."

Adverbs never inflect. They can appear after the verb or in other places in the sentence (see discussion of "word order" in this text).

Adverbs of manner

Adverbs of manner answer the question "how (in what way)" or "how much"?

In Yiddish, adverbs can be formed from adjectives by their taking on the base forms. These never inflect. Note: Not all adjectives can form adverbs (example: other).

Examples:

He reads **well**.	.ער לייענט גוט
She eats **nicely**.	.זי עסט שיין

In the first sentence, גוט does not modify ער but rather answers the question: *in what manner* does he read? In this usage, גוט is the equivalent to the English "well" (i.e. good*ly*).

In the second sentence, שיין answers the question: *in what manner* does she eat? Here שיין functions like the English "nicely."

Yiddish also has adverbs that are not formed from adjectives. They do not inflect.

Vocabulary: examples of adverbs

Adverb	Translation
אַזוי	so, meaning “so much” or “like this” (not “therefore”)
טאַקע	really, truly
שוין	already

Examples:

I sleep/am sleeping **so** well. איך שלאָף **אַזוי** גוט.
He is **really/truly** happy. ער איז **טאַקע** פֿריילעך.
They are **already** writing. זיי שרײַבן **שוין**.

Yiddish adverbs of time and place

Adverbs of time answer the question “when” while adverbs of place answer the question “where”?

Vocabulary: examples of adverbs of time and place

Adverb	Translation
איצט	now
דאָ	here

Examples:

He reads **now**. ער לייענט **איצט**.
She eats **here**. זי עסט **דאָ**.

In the first sentence, **איצט** answers the question: *when* does he read? In the second sentence, **דאָ** answers the question: *where* does she eat?

There are many other ways of forming adverbs in Yiddish, such as from uninflected participles as certain suffixes on nouns. These are presented in Unit 23 of this text.

The position of adverbs in a sentence varies. If it is an adverb of manner that provides information about a verb, it tends to follow the inflected form. Adverbs of time and place can be positioned away from the verb.

Adjective quantifiers

Adjective quantifiers appear directly before predicate adjectives. They do not inflect.

זייער can also appear before attributive adjectives.

Vocabulary: examples of adjective quantifiers

Adjective quantifiers	Translation
אַ ביסל	a little
זייער	very

Examples:

She is a little happy. — זי איז **אַ ביסל** פֿריילעך.
One reads/is reading very nicely. — מען לייענט **זייער** שיין.

Note the position of זייער in the predicate:
זייער follows the definite article but precedes the indefinite article.

She is very good. — זי איז זייער גוט.
She is a very good one (person). — זי איז זייער אַ גוטע.
She is the very good mother. — זי איז די זייער גוטע מאַמע.
She is a very good mother. — זי איז זייער אַ גוטע מאַמע.

Exercise 4.1

Locate the adverb(s) in each sentence. Then translate each sentence into English.

Example:

זי שלאָפֿט טאַקע גוט.

Adverbs: *טאַקע, גוט*
Translation: *She sleeps really well.*

1. די מענטשן לייענען אַלע שוין.
2. דו עסט אַזוי שיין.
3. מיר שלאָפֿן גוט.
4. איך בין איצט דאָ.
5. די מאַמע ווערט זייער אַ פֿריילעכע.

Exercise 4.2

Translate each sentence in 4.1 into Yiddish.

Example:

She sleeps very well. *זי שלאָפֿט זייער גוט.*

1. They read truly well.
2. I eat happily.
3. She is writing now.
4. You (plural) are a little small.
5. We are all very happy people.

UNIT 5
Numbers

Yiddish numbers

Yiddish numbers are written like roman numerals (not right-to-left like Yiddish script).

There is an alternative counting system based on the Hebrew alphabet (where, for example, 1 = א ,2 = ב, and so on) that will not be covered here.

Cardinal, or counting, numbers

(not part of this text's working vocabulary)

		צען	10	נול	0
		עלף	11	*איין-איינס	1
צוואַנציק	20	צוועלף	12	צוויי	2
דרײַסיק	30	דרײַצן	13	דרײַ	3
פֿערציק	40	פֿערצן	14	פֿיר	4
פֿופֿציק	50	פֿופֿצן	15	פֿינף/פֿינעף	5
זעכציק	60	זעכצן	16	זעקס	6
זיבעציק	70	זיבעצן	17	זיבן	7
אַכציק	80	אכצן	18	אַכט	8
נײַנציק	90	נײַנצן	19	נײַן	9

*For the number "1": איינס is used when counting, איין is used in all other cases.

Except for the number "1" in Yiddish, the forms of the cardinal numbers used for counting are identical to those used as adjectives. Yiddish cardinal numbers do not decline.

Thus, here is how one counts from one to five in Yiddish:

איינס, צוויי, דרײַ, פֿיר, פֿינף/פֿינעף.

The number "1," which is a counting number and does not describe how many there are of a specific noun, is איינס.

However, when modifying a noun, it appears as follows:

one person איין מענטש
one mother איין מאַמע
one book איין בוך

In order to make a number between 20 and 99, the following formulation is used: the number in the second digit position (ones column) is placed first, followed by the word און "and," with the number in the first digit (tens column) placed last.

Examples:

21 = "1 and 20" איין און צוואַנציק
57 = "7 and 50" זיבן און פֿופֿציק
99 = "9 and 90" נײַן און נײַנציק

Numbers over 99

הונדערט	100
טויזנט	1,000
מיליאָן	1,000,000

To make a number higher than 99: the number in the column furthest to the right (ones column) appears before the digit in the tens column, retaining the same rule as above.

Examples:

1952 = 1,000 + 900 + 2 + 50 טויזנט נײַן הונטערט צוויי און פֿופֿציק

A note regarding the numbers "100" and "1,000":

one hundred הונדערט
approximately one hundred אַ הונדערט

Ordinal numbers

Ordinal numbers are used to indicate the rank or position of a noun in a set. Ordinals do not appear in their base form in Yiddish. Rather, they decline using the same endings as attributive adjectives.

-ערשט	1st
-צווייט	2nd
-דריט	3rd
-פֿערט	4th
-פֿינפֿט	5th
-זעקסט	6th
-זיבעט	7th
-אַכט	8th
-נײַנט	9th
-צענט	10th

For the numbers 11–19, ordinal numbers are formed by adding the letter ט onto the cardinal number.

-עלפֿט 11th

For numbers 20 and higher, ordinal numbers are formed by adding the letters סט onto the cardinal number.

-צוואַנציקסט 20th
-נײַן און נײַנציקסט 99th

Examples:

He is the first person. ער איז דער **ערשטער** מענטש.
He is the ninety-ninth (person). ער איז דער **נײַן און נײַנציקסטער**.

Exercise 5.1

Provide each Yiddish cardinal number with its corresponding arabic number.

Example:

אַכט. *8*

1. פֿערצן
2. זיבן און צוואַנציק
3. הונדערט איין און פֿופֿציק
4. דרײַ
5. נײַן און זעכציק

Exercise 5.2

Provide each arabic number with the corresponding Yiddish cardinal number.

Example:

125 = הונדערט פֿינף און צוואַנציק

1. 333
2. 17
3. 1
4. 1,978
5. 1,568,212

Exercise 5.3

Translate the following phrases into Yiddish.

1. 6 books
2. 1 mother
3. the second person
4. 99 people
5. the fifty-eighth book

UNIT 6

Possessive pronouns

A possessive pronoun answers the question: whose X is it?

Possessive pronouns placed before a noun (in the same position as an article) inflect only in the plural. They retain the same form regardless of gender or case.

Possessive pronouns

Translation	Yiddish	Person
my	מײַן	First person singular
your	דײַן	Second person singular
his	זײַן	Third person singular masculine
her	איר	Third person singular feminine
our	אונדזער	First person plural
your	אײַער	Second person plural
their	זייער	Third person plural
whose	וועמענס	Interrogative pronoun

If the possessive pronoun is modifying a noun that is plural, the letter ע is added to the end of the pronoun:

Translation	Modifying a plural noun	Modifying a singular noun
my	מײַנע	מײַן
your	דײַנע	דײַן
his	זײַנע	זײַן
her	אירע	איר

Translation	Modifying a plural noun	Modifying a singular noun
our	אונדזערע	אונדזער
your	אײַערע	אײַער
their	זייערע	זייער

Examples:

Translation	Plural	Translation	Singular	Gender
my people	**מײַנע** מענטשן	my person	מײַן מענטש	masculine
my mothers	**מײַנע** מאַמעס	my mother	מײַן מאַמע	feminine
my books	**מײַנע** ביכער	my book	מײַן בוך	neuter

Note: Possessive pronouns function like indefinite articles as far as the declension of adjectives in the neuter-singular is concerned.

Thus:

The good book דאָס גוט**ע** בוך
A good book אַ גוט בוך
My good book מײַן גוט בוך

Note: To avoid repetition or when the context is clear, the Yiddish definite articles can be used in the place of possessive pronouns. Thus, if it has been established that one is referring to "my mother," one can refer to her as "די מאַמע".

Possessive pronouns in the predicate

In the predicate, possessive pronouns do decline: they inflect according to gender, number and case.

Examples:

The person is ours. דער מענטש איז אונדזער**ער**.
The mother is his. די מאַמע איז זײַנ**ע**.
The book is theirs. דאָס בוך איז זייער**ס**.
The books are yours. די ביכער זײַנען אײַער**ע**.

A possessive pronoun can also precede the noun being possessed. It is followed by the indefinite article and agrees with the noun it possesses in gender, number and case.

Examples:

A class of hers is here./There is a class of hers. אירער אַ קלאַס איז דאָ.

Exercise 6.1

Provide the correct ending on the possessive pronoun in each noun phrase. Then translate each one into English.

1. איר____ בוך
2. זייער____ מאַמעס
3. אונדזער____ מענטש
4. דיַינ____ ביכער
5. איַיער____ מענטשן

Exercise 6.2

Identify the gender (masculine, feminine, or neuter) and number (singular or plural) of each noun below. All of the nouns on this list are in the nominative case.

Then provide the correct form of the possessive adjectives and attributive adjectives indicated and translate the phrase into English.

Reminder: while attributive adjectives decline according to gender, number and case, possessive adjectives inflect only according to gender (singular-plural).

Example:

Noun	Attributive adjective	Possessive adjective
מענטשן	*גוט*	*מיַין*

Answer: masculine, plural

My good people מיַינע גוטע מענטשן

Noun	Attributive adjective	Possessive adjective	
ביכער	שיין	זיַין	1
מענטש	גרויס	אונדזער	2
מאַמע	פֿריילעך	זייער	3
מאַמעס	גוט	דיַין	4
בוך	קליין	איר	5

Exercise 6.3

Break down each sentence into its component parts, including the pronoun, verb, article or possessive pronoun, attributive adjective, and noun. Then render the sentence in the plural.

Reminder: Predicate adjectives do not change forms.

Example:

זײַן בוך איז גרויס.

Possessive adjective: singular = *זײַן*
Noun: neuter, singular, nominative = בוך
Verb in the present indicative: third person, singular = *איז*
Predicate adjective = גרויס
Sentence in the plural: ***זייערע ביכער זײַנען*** *גרויס.*

1. מײַן גרויס בוך איז גוט.
2. זײַן מאַמע לייענט שיין.
3. דאָס שיינע בוך ווערט מײַנס.
4. איך ווער אַ פֿרייליכער מענטש.
5. דו ביסט איר מאַמע.

Exercise 6.4

Translate the sentences in exercise 6.3 into English, first in their original forms and then in their plural forms.

Exercise 6.5

Translate the following sentences into Yiddish.

1. Their mother is eating happily.
2. My book is so good!
3. Our mother sleeps well.
4. His people write a little.
5. A class of mine is really good.

UNIT 7

Negation

Negation refers to the process of turning an affirmative statement into its opposite.

Example:

Affirmative statement: I am happy.
Negated statement: I am **not** happy.

Vocabulary: negation

Translation	Yiddish
Yes	יאָ
Not (dialect variants)	ניט - נישט*
No	ניין
(Not) any, none, no (one)	קיין

*Both dialect variants are provided here: this text employs ניט.

Negation of verbs

In order to negate a sentence, the negative particle, ניט, follows the conjugated verb.

Examples:

She is sleeping. זי שלאָפֿט.
She is not sleeping. זי שלאָפֿט **ניט**.

Note the placement of ניט after the conjugated verb. If the verb is followed by an adjective, the position of ניט remains the same. Exceptions to this rule regarding the position of ניט will be discussed in subsequent units on Yiddish word order.

Examples:

I am good.	איך בין גוט.
I am not good.	איך בין **ניט** גוט.

Negation of nouns

When negating a noun, the negative particle ניט follows the conjugated verb.

If the noun is preceded by the definite article "the," the negative particle appears after the verb. The article remains unchanged.

Examples:

The person is the mother.	דער מענטש איז די מאַמע.
The person is **not** the mother.	דער מענטש איז **ניט** די מאַמע.

Because it is dealing with a specific (the particular) mother, the sentence indicates that it is *this* mother that is being negated. That is, the person is not *this* particular mother (but could still be *a* mother).

The particle קיין

If the noun is indefinite (preceded by the article "a", or no article in the plural), the קיין particle appears in the place of an article before any noun that is not the subject of the verb.

The קיין appears along with the particle ניט: this does not create a "double negative" in Yiddish. In this function, קיין does not inflect.

Examples:

The person is a mother.	דער מענטש איז **אַ** מאַמע.
The person is not a (any) mother.	דער מענטש **ניט קיין** מאַמע.

Because the sentence is dealing with the category of "mother" rather than this particular mother, the whole category of "mother" is being negated. The use of קיין is akin to the English "any," as in "There isn't **any** mother here." It is impossible to have a negative form of a noun preceded by the indefinite article אַ or אַן: the article will always be replaced by קיין.

A noun in the indefinite plural is likewise preceded by קיין, even though there is no אַ or אַן.

Examples:

The people are mothers. די מענטשן זײַנען מאַמעס.
The people are not (any) mothers. די מענטשן זײַנען **ניט קיין** מאַמעס.

Other uses of the particle קיין

קיין carries a general meaning of "not any," "none" or "no one." When it functions as a pronoun, it inflects for case as a masculine adjective (see the third example, below). It is used with the particle ניט.

Examples:

The person reads/is not reading. דער מענטש לייענט **ניט**.
No person reads/is reading. קיין מענטש לייענט **ניט**.
No one reads/is reading. קיינ**ער** לייענט **ניט**.

Negation of existence/presence

The concept of existence/presence (versus non-existence or absence) is represented by the following idiomatic constructions:

Negative	Positive	
עס איז ניטאָ	עס איז דאָ	Singular
There is not	*There is*	
עס זײַנען ניטאָ	עס זײַנען דאָ	Plural
There are not	*There are*	

Examples:

There is a book. עס איז דאָ אַ בוך.
There is no book. עס איז ניטאָ קיין בוך.
There are books. עס זײַנען דאָ ביכער.
There are no books. עס זײַנען ניטאָ קיין ביכער.

The forms ניטאָ – דאָ are also used to indicate existence or presence for nouns.

Examples:

He is present. ער איז דאָ.
He is absent. ער איז ניטאָ.

Tips on how to negate: two sample sentences

1. זי איז די מאַמע.
2. זי איז אַ מאַמע.

1. Locate the conjugated verb: **איז**
2. Place the **ניט** after the conjugated verb: **זי איז ניט**
3. Look for nouns. If a noun is preceded by the definite article (**דער, די, דאָס**), it remains.

   Example: sentence 1 (above)

   זי איז ניט די מאַמע.

   Translation: She is not the (specific) mother.
4. If a noun is preceded by an indefinite article (**אַ, אַן**) or no article in the plural, the **קיין** stands in for the article.

   Example: sentence 2 (above).

   זי איז ניט קיין מאַמע.

   Translation: She is not a (any) mother.

Exercise 7.1

Negate each of the following sentences. Reminder: The **ניט** particle follows the conjugated verb.

Example:

My mother eats/is eating well.	מײַן מאַמע עסט גוט.
*My mother does not eat/is **not** eating well.*	*מײַן מאַמע עסט **ניט** גוט.*

1. דער מענטש עסט.
2. זי לייענט איצט.
3. זיי ווערן גרויס.
4. איך שלאָף גוט.
5. מיר שרײַבן שיין.

Exercise 7.2

Translate the sentences in exercise 7.1 into English, first in their original forms and then in their negated forms.

Exercise 7.3

Negate each of the following sentences. Reminder: The indefinite article requires the particle קיין as article, both in singular and plural. If there is an indefinite article, "a," "an," it will not appear in the negative form.

Examples:

Singular	*Plural*
1. זי איז די גוטע מאַמע.	*3. זיי זײַנען די גוטע מאַמעס.*
זי איז ניט די גוטע מאַמע.	*זי זײַנען ניט די גוטע מאַמעס.*
2. זי איז אַ גוטע מאַמע.	*4. זיי זײַנען גוטע מאַמעס.*
זי איז ניט קיין גוטע מאַמע.	*זי זײַנען ניט קיין גוטע מאַמעס.*

1. ער ווערט דער גוטער מענטש.
2. ער ווערט אַ גוטער מענטש.
3. זיי ווערן די גוטע מענטשן.
4. זיי ווערן גוטע מענטשן.
5. אונדזער מאַמע איז די שיינע.
6. אונדזער מאַמע איז אַ שיינע.
7. אונדזערע מאַמעס זײַנען די שיינע.
8. אונדזערע מאַמעס זײַנען שיינע.

Exercise 7.4

Translate the sentences in exercises 7.3 into English, first in their original forms and then in their negated forms.

Exercise 7.5

Translate the following sentences into Yiddish.

1. He is not a happy person.
2. This book is not so good.
3. Their mother is not very nice.
4. Our book is not really small.
5. We are not the small people.

UNIT 8

Yiddish word order 1: verb position, direct questions, the second person conjugation of the imperative mood (direct commands)

Introduction to Yiddish word order

Yiddish word order is governed by certain rules that determine how the parts of a sentence can be arranged. The term often used to describe parts of a Yiddish sentence is the *sentence unit*, which refers to any word or group of words that work together to perform a given syntactical function. A sentence unit might include: the subject of the sentence with its accompanying adjectives and adverbs; the conjugated verb; the infinitive of a verb; a past participle; the object and its accompanying articles, adjectives; adverbs; and so on. A sentence unit can be a single word, a string of words that belong together, or a clause. Yiddish includes the following sentence units: subject; inflected verb; uninflected verb (fixed part of a verb such as an infinitive or participle); predicate; direct object; indirect object; adverbs of time, place, manner; clauses, and some other constructions.

"Normal" word order in Yiddish is S-V-O: subject-conjugated verb-object. However, many other permutations are possible, provided that certain rules are followed. In these cases, word order can help to emphasize certain elements in a sentence, in particular when a word other than the subject appears in the first position.

Verb position

There is one unbreakable rule in Yiddish word order: the inflected verb occupies the second position.

An inflected verb appears in the first position in three cases only:

(1) a "yes/no" question;
(2) a direct command (imperative mood);
(3) an implied causal relationship: "so/therefore" (these will be outlined more fully below and in future units).

The fixed (uninflected) part of the verb forms its own sentence unit and does not appear in the second position. Verbs with an inflected and fixed part will be treated in future units.

Example:

1 2 3
די גוטע מאַמע | איז | אַ שיינער מענטש.

The good mother is a nice person.

This sentence contains three sentence units:

The subject: די גוטע מאַמע
The inflected verb: איז
The object (in this case, a predicate): אַ שיינער מענטש

The following sentence would also be correct:

1 2 3
אַ שיינער מענטש | איז | די גוטע מאַמע.

The good mother is *a nice person*. (Emphasis in the Yiddish by putting it in the first position.)

Note: The inflected verb remains in the second position in the sentence.

Adverbs and word order

Adverbs in Yiddish are very mobile: they can appear in almost any position except the second position (which belongs to the inflected verb).

Adverbs of manner tend to follow the inflected verb they are modifying.

Examples:

He writes well now.	ער שרײַבט גוט איצט.
He writes well now.	ער שרײַבט איצט גוט.
Now he writes well.	איצט שרײַבט ער גוט.

Direct questions

The "normal" position of the inflected verb is in the second position. One way to form a question is to place the inflected verb in the first position of the sentence. This creates a "yes/no" question. Alternately, the particle

צי can be placed in the first position as a placeholder. צי does not change the meaning of the sentence.

Example:

	3 2 1
The person is nice/attractive.	דער מענטש | איז | שיין.

This is a statement.

To make it into a question, the verb is placed in the first position. This is called *inversion*.

	3 2 1
Is the person nice/attractive?	איז | דער מענטש | שיין?

The answer to this form of question is generally "yes" or "no." It is not an open-ended question.

Note: In the process of inversion, the inflected verb has simply switched positions with the subject of the verb.

Even in cases where the original sentence does not use subject-verb-object order (i.e. the sentence does not begin with the subject of the verb), the subject of the verb will appear second in the question.

Example:

	3 2 1
The person is *nice/attractive*.	שיין | איז | דער מענטש.
Is the person nice/attractive?	איז | דער מענטש | שיין?

When forming "yes/no" questions in the second person singular, the inflected verb and personal pronoun contract as follows:

סטו = דו + סט + *base of verb*

For example:

Translation	Question (first position)	Translation	Declarative (second position)
Are you?	ביסטו?	You are	דו ביסט
Are you sleeping/ do you sleep?	שלאָפֿסטו?	You sleep/ are sleeping	דו שלאָפֿסט

All other forms of the verb remain the same, and the question is indicated by inversion alone: the placing of the inflected verb in the first position.

Examples:

"yes-no" question	Declarative statement
שלאָף איך?	איך שלאָף
שלאָפֿסטו?	דו שלאָפֿסט
שלאָפֿט ער?	ער שלאָפֿט
שלאָפֿט זי?	זי שלאָפֿט
שלאָפֿט עס?	עס שלאָפֿט
שלאָפֿט מען?	מען שלאָפֿט
שלאָפֿן מיר?	מיר שלאָפֿן
שלאָפֿט איר?	איר שלאָפֿט
שלאָפֿן זיי?	זיי שלאָפֿן

Forming direct, open-ended (non-"yes/no") questions in Yiddish

Yiddish questions can be formed by placing question words (interrogative pronouns) before the verb.

Interrogative pronouns

Interrogative pronouns are pronouns used to ask questions. Like all pronouns, they refer to specific nouns.

Vocabulary: interrogative pronouns

Translation	Yiddish
what	וואָס
which declines according to number only	plural: וואָסערע singular: וואָסער
who	ווער

As discussed later in this text, the pronoun װער declines. װאָסער declines according to number only (singular and plural). The pronoun װאָס never declines.

Examples:

What is the person eating? װאָס עסט דער מענטש?
"What" replaces a noun like "banana."

Which people are eating? װאָסערע מענטשן עסן?
"Which" replaces a noun like "the hungry ones."

Who is eating? װער עסט?
"Who" replaces a noun like "people."

Question words

Yiddish also uses question words to ask open-ended questions. These do not refer to a specific noun.

Vocabulary: question words

Translation	Yiddish
where	װוּ
how	װי
how, in what way	װי אַזױ
how much, how many	װיפֿל
when	װען
why	פֿאַרװאָס
answer to "why": because (see unit on conjunctions)	װײַל

Examples of Yiddish questions and answers:

What is the person reading? — 1 **װאָס** לייענט דער מענטש?
The person is reading a book. — דער מענטש לייענט אַ בוך.

Which books does the person read? — 2 **װאָסערע** ביכער לייענט דער מענטש?
The person reads all books. — דער מענטש לייענט אַלע ביכער.

Where does the person read? — 3 **װוּ** לייענט דער מענטש?
The person reads here. — דער מענטש לייענט דאָ.

How does the person read? The person reads well.	4	**ווי** (אַזוי) לייענט דער מענטש? דער מענטש לייענט גוט.
How much does the person read? The person reads a little.	5	**וויפֿל** לייענט דער מענטש? דער מענטש לייענט אַ ביסל.
When does the person read? The person is reading now.	6	**ווען** לייענט דער מענטש? דער מענטש לייענט איצט.
Who reads/is reading the book? The person is reading the book.	7	**ווער** לייענט דאָס בוך? דער מענטש לייענט דאָס בוך.
Why is the person reading? Because the book is good.	8	**פֿאַרוואָס** לייענט דער מענטש? ווײַל דאָס בוך איז גוט.

The second person conjugation of the imperative mood (direct commands)

The second person conjugation of the imperative mood refers to a direct command made to a "you."

For example: Go! Eat! Stop!

In Yiddish, the direct command appears in the first position in the sentence. Along with direct questions, this is one of the cases where the inflected verb does not appear in the second position.

The second person conjugation of the imperative mood is formed in the singular by the base of the verb (with no ending) and in the plural by adding an ending of ט to the base form. The conjugation is formed from the base (infinitive without the endings ן or ען) + the endings indicated below.

The second person imperative conjugations

Translation	Example 2 זײַן	Example 1 לייענען	Ending on base	Form
1. Read! / 2. Be! (1 person, informal)	זײַ!	לייען!	–!	singular, informal
1. Read! / 2. Be! (plural, 1 person formal)	זײַט!	לייענט!	–ט!	plural/ formal

The particle זשע placed immediately after the verb serves as an intensifier.

Example:

Go on and eat! עס זשע!

Summary: basic rules of Yiddish word order

4+	3		2/3	2	1	0
whatever remains	the uninflected verb	**ניט**	any of the following: direct object pronoun, indirect object pronoun, adverbs of time and, place, subject noun, subject pronoun	the inflected verb*	any unit but the inflected verb*	non-unit words such as exclamations or conjunctions

*Exceptions: "yes/no" questions, commands.

Exercise 8.1

Place the inflected verb provided in {} into the correct position in each sentence. Do not alter the order of the rest of the sentence.

Note: The sentence units are separated by –.

Example:

מיר – דאָ. {לייענען}
מיר לייענען דאָ.

1. איך – ניט – דאָ. {בין}
2. מיר – אַלע – איצט. {שלאָפֿן}
3. די פֿריילעכע מענטשן – אַ ביסל. {עסן}
4. זי – טאַקע – אַ גוטע מאַמע. {ווערט}
5. מען – די גרויסע ביכער. {לייענט}
6. אונדזערע ביכער – ניט קיין גוטע. {זייַנען}
7. ער – אַזוי שיין. {איז}
8. איצט – איר. {שרייַבט}

Exercise 8.2

Translate the sentences in 8.1 into English.

Exercise 8.3

Render the sentences in 8.1 into "yes-no" questions.

Reminder: To make a "yes/no" question, simply switch the positions of the first and second sentence units so that the inflected verb appears first. The rest of the sentence remains unchanged.

Example:

מיר זײַנען דאָ.
זײַנען מיר דאָ?

Exercise 8.4

Translate the sentences in 8.3 into English.

Exercise 8.5

Translate the following sentences into Yiddish.

Reminder: Q.8–Q.10 are "yes/no" questions: inflected verb first!

1. When do you eat?
2. Why is she here?
3. Who are the people?
4. Read the great book!
5. What does it eat?
6. How much do the mothers sleep?
7. Where am I?
8. Do you write/are you (singular, informal form) writing?
9. Are the books ours?
10. Am I here?

Exercise 8.6

Provide the singular/informal and plural/formal forms of the second person conjugation of the imperative mood for the verbs listed below.

Example:

ווערן: ווער! ווערט!

1. לייענען
2. עסן
3. שרײַבן
4. זײַן

UNIT 9

Yiddish word order 2: conjunctions, relative pronouns, relative clauses, consecutive word order ("so")

Conjunctions

Conjunctions are the part of speech that links two words, clauses or sentences together.

As far as Yiddish word order is concerned, they are non-unit words (a position of "0") that begin word order anew from 1.

Example:

3	2	1	**0**	3	2	1
.אַ ביסל	שרײַבט	זי	**און**	אַ בוך	לייענט	די מאַמע

Translation: The mother is reading a book **and** she is writing a little.
Conjunctions fall into different categories.

1. Coordinating conjunctions: these link two clauses together that have equal emphasis.

Vocabulary: examples of coordinating conjunctions

Translation	Conjunction
but	אָבער
or	אָדער
and	און

Examples:

He is small **but** he is becoming great. ער איז קליין **אָבער** ער ווערט גרויס.
Is she sleeping **or** is she reading? שלאָפֿט זי **אָדער** לייענט זי?

2. Subordinating conjunctions: these join a subordinate clause to a main clause, with the emphasis on the main clause.

Vocabulary: examples of subordinating conjunctions

Translation	Conjunction
if, whether	אויב
that, when	אַז
until	ביז
because	ווײַל
although	כאָטש
*so, therefore	טאָ*

*Only used with questions and commands.

Examples:

I do not read/am not reading **if** he sleeps/is sleeping. — איך לייען ניט **אויב** ער שלאָפֿט.

I do not read/am not reading **because** he is sleeping. — איך לייען ניט **ווײַל** ער שלאָפֿט.

Note: Subordinate clauses that precede a main clause are treated as single sentence units. This means that the inflected verb in the second, main clause must appear first so that it retains its position as the second sentence unit. Thus:

If he is sleeping, I don't read. — אויב ער שלאָפֿט, **לייען** איך ניט.

3. Correlative conjunctions: these are pairs of conjunctions that work in tandem.

Vocabulary: examples of correlative conjunctions

Translation	Conjunction
either...or	סײַ... סײַ

Example:

Either he sleeps/is sleeping or he eats/is eating. — סײַ ער שלאָפֿט, סײַ ער עסט.

Relative pronouns

The Yiddish question words also serve as relative pronouns. When they link two sentences together they behave like conjunctions. They do not decline.

Example:

I do not eat **when** I read. איך עס ניט **ווען** איך לייען.

Relative clauses

A relative clause that refers to a subject or direct object noun is linked to the sentence by the pronoun וואָס, with וואָס meaning: that, whom or which. It does not decline.

Example:

The person **who** is reading is nice/attractive. דער מענטש **וואָס** לייענט איז שיין.

Here "who וואָס" refers back to "the person דער מענטש."

Note: A full discussion of this topic is beyond the scope of this text.

Consecutive word order: "so"

In Yiddish, the conjunction "so" generally does not appear as a word in the sense of "therefore" in declarative sentences (statements of fact). Rather, "so/therefore" is implied through the position of the inflected verb in the second clause.

In these constructions, subordinate clauses that precede a main clause are treated as single sentence units: the inflected verb in the main clause must appear first so that it remains the second sentence unit.

To make the statement "A therefore B," the inflected verb in the main B clause is placed in the first position in the second clause. This is called "consecutive word order."

Example:

B: MAIN CLAUSE (THE RESULT) = INFLECTED VERB IN FIRST POSITION	*implied therefore*	A: SUBORDINATE CLAUSE (THE CAUSE)
שלאָף איך.		דו שרײַבסט,

Translation: You are writing **so I am sleeping**.

To reiterate: There is no word in Yiddish to express the cause-effect relationship between two clauses in a declarative sentence. The words אַז or טאָ should not be used in this function. This relationship is expressed using word order. The adverb דערפֿאַר, "therefore" or "then," can be used to introduce a new sentence or follow a conjunction in Yiddish.

The exception to consecutive word order: "so/therefore" in a question or command

The conjunction טאָ is used with the meaning of "so, therefore" only when the verb already appears as the first sentence unit.

1. In questions

Question	Declarative statement
דו ביסט גוט **טאָ** לייענסטו?	דו ביסט גוט, **לייענסט** דו.
You are good **so** you read?	You are good **so** you read.

2. In the imperative mood

Imperative mood	Declarative statement
דו ביסט גוט **טאָ** לייען!	דו ביסט גוט, **לייענסט** דו.
You are good **so** read!	You are good **so** you read.

Note: Consecutive word order is often used when telling a story in Yiddish: it serves to move the story forward through the use of an implied "so."

Exercise 9.1

Create a sentence by linking sentence 1 from column א with the sentence 1 from column ג by means of any conjunction from column ב. Choose any conjunction that makes sense in the sentence (see the example below). Then do the same for sentences 2–5. Create as many versions of each sentence as possible.

Example:

זי איז שיין **אָבער/אָדער/אויב/און/ביז/ווײַל/כאָטש** *זי איז ניט קיין גוטע.*
She is pretty **but/or/if/and/until/because/although** *she is not a good one (woman).*

ג	ב	א	
זי איז ניט קיין גוטע.	אָבער	זי איז שיין.	1
איך עס.	אָדער	איך לייען.	2
מען שרײַבט ניט.	אויב	מען לייענט אַ בוך.	3
זיי זײַנען ניטאָ.	און	מיר זײַנען דאָ.	4
איך לייען איצט.	ביז	דאָס בוך איז גוט.	5
	ווײַל		
	כאָטש		

Exercise 9.2

Translate your sentences from 9.1 into English.

Exercise 9.3

ג	ב	א	
זי איז ניט קיין גוטע.	"so" using consecutive word order	זי איז שיין.	1
איך עס.		איך לייען.	2
מען שרײַבט ניט.		מען לייענט אַ בוך.	3
זיי זײַנען ניטאָ.		מיר זײַנען דאָ.	4
איך לייען איצט.		דאָס בוך איז גוט.	5

Using the chart above, create three sentences with a causal connection between sentence 1 from column **א** and sentence 1 from column **ג** above using "consecutive word order." That is, the sentence from column **א** should be followed by a comma (,) and the conjugated verb from column **ג** should follow immediately after the comma.

Repeat with sentences 2–5.

Example (sentence 1):

זי איז שיין, איז זי ניט קיין גוטע.

She is pretty ***so*** *she is not a good one (woman).*

Exercise 9.4

Translate your sentences from 9.3 into English.

UNIT 10

Irregular infinitives: *to have* האָבן, and others

Irregular infinitives

A number of Yiddish verbs have irregular infinitives. That is, their infinitives are different from their base forms in the present indicative tense and imperative mood conjugations.

The verb to have *האָבן*

The verb האָבן conjugates irregularly in the present indicative tense.
Here is the conjugation:

Translation	Conjugated form	Person, number
I have	איך האָב	First person singular
You have	דו האָסט	Second person singular
He/she/it/one has	ער/זי/עס/מען האָט	Third person singular
We have	מיר האָבן	First person plural
You have	איר האָט	Second person plural
They have	זיי האָבן	Third person plural

Note: In Yiddish, the verb *to have* האָבן (along with the verb זײַן) is essential to forming the past tense, where it acts as the auxiliary (helping verb) along with a past participle form.

Example:

I **read/was reading** a book. איך האָב **געלייענט** אַ בוך.

Other verbs with irregular infinitives

Aside from *to be* זײַן and *to have* האָבן, Yiddish has a number of other verbs whose base forms are different from their infinitive forms. Note the irregularities in conjugation in the present indicative tense as well as the second person conjugations of the imperative mood.

Here are a few examples:

געבן	וויסן	טאָן	Infinitive
to give	to know information	to do	meaning
גיב–	וויס–	טו–	*base of verb* infinitive minus ending of ן, ען
Present tense conjugations			Person, number, personal pronoun
גיב	וויס	טו	First person singular איך
גיסט	ווייסט	טוסט	Second person singular דו
גיט	וויס(ט)*	טוט	Third person singular ער/זי/עס/מען
גיבן	ווייסן	טוען	First person plural מיר
גיט	ווייסט	טוט	Second person plural איר
גיבן	ווייסן	טוען	Third person plural זיי
Second person conjugations of the imperative mood			
גיב!	**	טו!	singular, informal
גיט!	**	טוט!	plural/formal

*Both alternative forms exist for this verb.
**One cannot logically command someone to "know".

Exercise 10.1

Conjugate the following irregular verbs in the present tense as well as the second person conjugation of the imperative mood:

1. געבן
2. האָבן
3. ווייסן
4. זײַן (review from a previous unit)
5. טאָן

Exercise 10.2

Provide the missing form of the verb provided in {} in each number to match the subject.

Make sure that the form agrees with the subject of the verb in each sentence in person and number.

Note that numbers 8–10 are in the imperative mood (indicated by !)

Example:

די מאַמעס _______ {האָבן}.

די מאַמעס האָבן = third person plural

1. עס _______ {געבן}.
2. מען _______ {טאָן}.
3. _______ {האָבן} איר?
4. די מאַמע _______ {וויסן}.
5. דו _______ {געבן}.
6. אַלע מענטשן _______ {געבן}.
7. איך _______ {וויסן}.
8. (second person singular) _______ {געבן}!
9. (second person plural) _______ {טאָן}!
10. (second person plural) _______ {האָבן}!

Exercise 10.3

Translate your answers from 10.2 into English.

Example:

The mothers have   *די מאַמעס האָבן*

UNIT 11

The accusative case, declension of proper names

The accusative case

The accusative case refers to a noun (and its accompanying article/adjective) or a pronoun that is acting as the direct object of the verb.

For example:

The happy person is reading the good book.	דער פֿריילעכער מענטש לייענט דאָס גוטע בוך.

Who is the "doer" of the verb, i.e. who is doing the action of reading?

Answer: the happy person (nominative)

The happy person is *verb*-ing (in this case, reading) + *what* or *whom* (direct object)?

Answer: the good book. "The good book" is the direct object and is in the accusative case.

Although this noun phrase (the article does not look any different from the nominative case, it is accusative because of its function in the sentence as the direct object of the verb. Both feminine and neuter noun phrases in the accusative case remain identical in form to the nominative case. Noun phrases in the masculine do take on a different form in the accusative from their nominative forms.

Here is an example using the noun, בריוו, *letter*, which is masculine in gender.

The happy person is reading **the good letter**.	דער פֿריילעכער מענטש לייענט **דעם גוטן בריוו**.

Who is the "doer" of the verb, i.e. who is doing the action of reading?

Answer: the happy person (nominative)

The happy person is *verb*-ing (in this case, reading) + *what* or *whom* (direct object)?

Answer: the good letter. "The good letter" is the direct object and is in the accusative case.

In a sentence where it acts as the doer of the verb (and thus be in the nominative case), the phrase "the good letter" would inflect as follows:

The good letter is happy. **דער** גוטער בריוו איז פֿריילעך.

In the accusative case, the noun phrase "the good letter" takes on a different form of the word "the" and a different ending on the adjective "good" from the nominative case.

Note: Although contemporary English does not have a full case system, it does maintain some elements of the accusative case: You see **me**, she sees **him**, he sees **her**.

Forming the accusative case

In the masculine singular, the accusative case takes different endings on its definite article and adjectives than in the nominative case. The feminine, neuter, and plural forms in the accusative case remain the same forms as the nominative case. However, all accusative nouns or noun phrases that serve as direct objects are in the accusative case: what makes them accusative is their function in relation to the noun.

Reminder: With a few exceptions (proper names and a handful of nouns such as "father"), nouns do not inflect for case. Their forms change only in the plural. Rather, it is the word "the" and the attributive adjective in a noun phrase that decline.

Accusative case

Example with adjective גוט	Accusative ending on adjective base *direct object*	Example with adjective גוט	Nominative ending on adjective base *subject*	
דעם גוטן אַ גוטן	דעם ־ן אַ ־ן	דער גוטער אַ גוטער	דער ־ער אַ ־ער	Masculine
די גוטע אַ גוטע	די ־ע אַ ־ע	די גוטע אַ גוטע	די ־ע אַ ־ע	Feminine
דאָס גוטע	דאָס ־ע	דאָס גוטע	דאָס ־ע	Neuter definite
אַ גוט	אַ –	אַ גוט	אַ –	Neuter indefinite
די גוטע גוטע	די ־ע ־ע	די גוטע גוטע	די ־ע ־ע	Plural

Note: As in the nominative case, the definite ("the") and indefinite ("a") forms of adjectives are identical except in the neuter gender.

Endings on adjective bases

Adjectives linked with the article דעם generally take the ending ן–.

Examples:

דעם גרויסן, דעם גוטן

Exceptions to endings

(only קליין forms part of this text's working vocabulary)

Translation	Examples	Ending of	Adjective base ending in:
small	דעם קליינעם	–עם	–נ
religiously observant	דעם פֿרומען	–ען	–מ
blue	דעם בלאָען	–ען	a vowel
raw	דעם רויען	–ען	a diphthong (וי, יי, ײַ)
new	דעם נײַעם	–עם	special case: נײַ

Declension of proper names

Proper names of people inflect when they are not in the nominative case. Most names take the ending ן–.

Example:

I am reading Shakespeare. איך לייען שעקספּירן.

Names ending in ם ,ן, a stressed vowel or a syllabic ל (a ל that functions as a vowel after a consonant) are given an ending of ען when not in the nominative case:

Examples:

Sam סעמען –ם
Goldstein גאָלדשטיינען –ן
Shai שײַען stressed vowel
Motl מאָטלען syllabic ל

Cases with examples in the nominative and accusative

Accusative *object*	Nominative *subject*	Gender/number example
דעם גוטן מענטש אַ גוטן מענטש	דער גוטער מענטש אַ גוטער מענטש	Masculine מענטש
די גוטע מאַמע אַ גוטע מאַמע	די גוטע מאַמע אַ גוטע מאַמע	Feminine מאַמע
דאָס גוטע בוך אַ גוט- בוך	דאָס גוטע בוך אַ גוט- בוך	Neuter בוך
די גוטע מענטשן/ מאַמעס/ביכער - גוטע מענטשן/ מאַמעס/ביכער	די גוטע מענטשן/ מאַמעס/ביכער - גוטע מענטשן/ מאַמעס/ביכער	Plural מענטשן מאַמעס ביכער

Tips on how to determine the case of a noun:

Sample sentence:

The mother is reading the book. די מאַמע לייענט דאָס בוך.

1. Find the verb.
   Verb: לייענט
2. Ask: who/what is the subject (doer) of the verb: who or what is doing the action? The doer of the action is in the nominative case.
   The form of the verb (ending of ט) indicates that the doer of the verb is either third person singular or second person plural.
   Subject of verb: די מאַמע = nominative case. It agrees with the verb (it is third person singular).
   Reminder: An object that follows verbs such as ווערן, זײַן is also in the nominative case.
3. Find the direct object, if any.
   Ask: the subject is *verb*-ing what, whom? The direct object is in the accusative case.
   Direct object: דאָס בוך = accusative case.

Exercise 11.1

Each form is provided in the nominative. Provide the gender and number as well as the accusative form.

Example:

דער גוטער מענטש *nominative*
דעם גוטן מענטש *masculine singular, accusative*

1. דאָס קליינע בוך
2. די גוטע מאַמע
3. אַ שיינער מענטש
4. גרויסע ביכער
5. די פֿריילעכע מענטשן

Exercise 11.2

Identify the form of the verb and noun phrases in the sentence.
Method:

1. Locate the verb. Provide its person (1, 2, 3) and number (singular, plural).
2. Ask: who is doing the verb? = nominative.
3. Ask: verb + what/whom (direct object)? = accusative.

For Q.2 and Q.3, provide the full noun phrase and indicate the gender and number.

Note: Not every sentence has a nominative and accusative; in some cases, the subject is implied in the verb form (Q.3 below) or there is a predicate nominative (Q.5 below).

Reminder: Not every Yiddish sentence has S-V-O word order (Q.8 below).

Example:

דער גוטער מענטש שרײַבט אַ גרויס בוך.

1. *Verb:* שרײַבט*; third person, singular.*
2. *Nominative:* דער גוטער מענטש*; masculine singular.*
3. *Accusative:* אַ גרויס בוך*; neuter singular.*

1. אונדזערע מאַמעס האָבן שיינע ביכער.
2. לייענסטו אַ שיין בוך?
3. איך האָב אַ גוטע מאַמע.
4. וואָס ווייס(ט) דער מענטש?
5. איך ווער אַ גוטער מענטש.

6. מען האָט דעם מענטש.
7. אַלע מענטשן האָבן מאַמעס.
8. ביכער האָט ער ניט!
9. איך לייען בערגעלסאָנען* — *The Soviet Yiddish author, Dovid Bergelson, masculine
10. זי האָט מאָטלען.* — *The name Motl, masculine

Exercise 11.3

Translate the sentences in 11.2 into English.

Example:

דער גוטער מענטש שרײַבט אַ גרויס בוך.

The good person writes/is writing a great/big book.

Exercise 11.4

Translate the following sentences into Yiddish.

1. I have no good books.
2. Who is the great person?
3. They have the small book.
4. We do not have a good person.
5. She has no mother.

UNIT 12
Prepositions, adverbs designating place

Prepositions

Prepositions are connecting words that express a relation between nouns or pronouns and other parts of a sentence.

For example:

I walk **under** the tree.
She speaks **with** her father.
We can't go **because of** work.
Let's talk **about** your family.
They went **without** their dog.
Do you want cookies **instead of** vegetables?
He read **to** his daughter.

All prepositions govern the *dative case*. This can be expressed as: preposition + *what/whom? = dative case.*

Example:

I read **with** my mother.
Question: I read **with** *what/whom*?
Answer: my mother. "My mother" is in the dative case.

The dative case has its own set of endings for articles and adjectives. The dative case will be presented in the next unit.

Vocabulary: examples of prepositions

Here is a list of a few prepositions for the purposes of example and practice, with their approximate English equivalents.

English equivalent(s)	Preposition
on, at, for, etc.	אויף
in	אין
at (someone's)	בײַ
about	וועגן
with	מיט
for/before/in front of	פֿאַר
from	פֿון
to	צו
to (a place)	קיין

Special idiomatic uses of Yiddish prepositions

Prepositions do not translate neatly from one language to another because the usage of prepositions tends to be highly idiomatic. Some of these idiomatic uses are presented below.

Prepositions and motion

Vocabulary of travel, places

Translation	Notes	Yiddish
to go/travel on foot (not by vehicle)	regular verb	גיין
home	feminine; plural form: היימען	היים
wedding	feminine; plural form: חתונות pronounced *khasene-khasenes*	חתונה
New York		ניו־יאָרק
to go/travel by vehicle (not on foot)	regular verb	פֿאָרן
class	masculine; plural form: קלאַסן	קלאַס
city	feminine; plural form: שטעט	שטאָט

1. To travel **to** any geographic location, named or unnamed, employs the preposition אין:

   We are traveling **to** a city. מיר פֿאָרן **אין** אַ שטאָט.

   To travel to any named geographic location can also employ the preposition קיין:

   We are traveling **to** New York. מיר פֿאָרן **אין** ניו־יאָרק.

   or

   We are traveling **to** New York. מיר פֿאָרן **קיין** ניו־יאָרק.

2. Verbs of remaining stationary, such as the verb זײַן, use the preposition אין:

   We are **in** a city. מיר זײַנען **אין** אַ שטאָט.
   We are **in** New York. מיר זײַנען **אין** ניו־יאָרק.

3. Being in/going to certain places employs the preposition **אין**, often without an article:

   in/to (the) class **אין** קלאַס

4. Note: home

   the home די היים
   at home **אין** דער היים
   (going to) home אַהיים

5. To be at/go to a special event, especially a ritual event, employs the preposition **אויף**:

   at/to a wedding **אויף** אַ חתונה

Other idiomatic uses of prepositions

1. To see/visit/stay with another person employs the preposition **בײַ** (it functions like the French *chez).*

   I eat **at** Motl**'s** (place). איך עס **בײַ** מאָטל**ען**.

2. To function in a language employs the preposition **אויף**:

   The book is **in** Yiddish. דאָס בוך איז **אויף** ייִדיש.

These are just a few examples. In general, usage of Yiddish prepositions should be learned as new vocabulary items when they are encountered.

Adverbs of location/motion

There are three different adverbs of location that correspond to the English forms: (1) here, (2) there, (3) where. In their base forms, these are stationary: they do not indicate motion or change of location.

Each of the three adverbs of location takes on different forms when it indicates motion, either after a preposition (to, from) or when there is a clear change of location. As adverbs, they do not decline.

HERE	THERE	WHERE	
דאָ	דאָרט/דאָרטן	וווּ	ADVERB OF LOCATION
here	*there*	*where*	*AT A PLACE: NO MOTION/ CHANGE OF LOCATION*
דאַנען	דאָרט/דאָרטן	וואַנען	PREPOSITION + PLACE
prep. + *here (hence)*	prep. + *there (hence)*	prep. + *where (whence)*	*TO/FROM/... + HERE/ THERE/WHERE*
אַהער	אַהין	וווּהין	ADVERB OF MOTION
to here (hither)	*to there (thence)*	*to where (whither)*	*PLACE TO WHICH*

Examples:

LOCATION	Where are you?	וווּ ביסטו?
LOCATION	I am here.	איך בין דאָ.
LOCATION	You are there.	דו ביסט דאָרט/דאָרטן.
PREPOSITION	From where (whence) are you?	פֿון וואַנען ביסטו?
PREPOSITION	I am from here (hence).	איך בין פֿון דאַנען.
PREPOSITION	You are from there (thence)	דו ביסט פֿון דאָרט/דאָרטן.
MOTION	Where (whither) are you going?	וווּהין גייסטו?
MOTION	You are coming here (hither).	דו גייסט אַהער.
MOTION	I am going there (thither).	איך גיי אַהין.

Exercise 12.1

Make sentences using the prepositions provided in {} to fill in the blanks. Each number will yield two sentences.

1–2. די מאַמע שרײַבט אַ בוך ______ ייִדיש. {אויף, וועגן}
3–4. מיר פֿאָרן ______ ניו־יאָרק. {אין, קיין}
5–6. די מענטשן זײַנען ______ מאָטלען. {בײַ, מיט}
7–8. דאָס בוך איז ______ מאָטלען. {פֿאַר, פֿון}

Exercise 12.2

Translate the Yiddish sentences from 12.1 into English.

Exercise 12.3

Translate the following sentences into English. Note the idiomatic uses of prepositions. Attempt to render your translations into idiomatic English (so they do not sound like translations).

1. מיר שלאָפֿן דאָ.
2. זיי זײַנען אין ניו־יאָרק און לייענען אַ בוך פֿון דאָרטן.
3. פֿאַרוואָס גייט איר ניט אויף קיין חתונה?
4. די מאַמע פֿאָרט אַהין צו מאָטלען.
5. וווּהין גייט ער?

Exercise 12.4

Translate the following sentences into Yiddish using the appropriate form of the preposition.

1. I am at home with Motl.
2. We are not going/traveling to New York to a (any) wedding.
3. She is not traveling (to) here: she is at Motl's (place).
4. You are writing a book for Motl.
5. They are going home (on foot).

UNIT 13

Indirect object, the dative case, declension of nouns, the dative as possessive case

Indirect object

The indirect object is governed by the *implied* prepositions "to" or "for." Indirect objects answer the questions: verb + *to/for what? to/for whom?*

For example:

The mother reads/is reading **the people** a book.	.די מאַמע לייענט די מענטשן אַ בוך

In Yiddish, indirect objects do not require the preposition "to" or "for." Instead, they are governed by the dative case (discussed below).

Note the parts of the above sentence:

verb = לייענט
subject of verb = nominative case = די מאַמע
direct object (reads + what/whom?) = accusative case = אַ בוך
indirect object (reads + to/for whom?) = dative case = די מענטשן

There are verbs that often impose the dative case, such as *to give (to someone)* געבן or *to write (to someone)* שרײַבן. Others include to believe (in someone), to tell (someone), to show (someone), to reply (to someone), to send (to someone), to write (to someone), and so on.

The dative case

The dative case has two functions in Yiddish:

1. It is the "prepositional case": the case of any noun or pronoun that follows a preposition.
2. It is the case of any indirect object.

As with all cases, the dative form has its own system of endings for definite articles and adjectives. The masculine, feminine, and neuter definite forms inflect in the dative case. The neuter indefinite and plural forms remain uninflected (i.e. in their nominative forms).

Nouns in the dative do not inflect for case. Rather, it is the word "the" and the attributive adjective in a noun phrase that decline.

The dative case

Example with adjective גוט	Dative ending on adjective base *preposition/ indirect object*	Example with adjective גוט	Nominative ending on adjective base *subject*	
דעם גוטן אַ גוטן	דעם –ן אַ –ן	דער גוטער אַ גוטער	דער –ער אַ –ער	Masculine
דער גוטער אַ גוטער	דער –ער אַ –ער	די גוטע אַ גוטע	די –ע אַ –ע	Feminine
דעם גוטן	דעם –ן	דאָס גוטע	דאָס –ע	Neuter definite
אַ גוט	אַ –	אַ גוט–	אַ –	Neuter indefinite
די גוטע גוטע	די –ע –ע	די גוטע גוטע	די –ע –ע	Plural

Contractions of prepositions and articles

In many instances, the article **דעם** is contracted with the preposition it follows.

For example:

אויף דעם – אויפֿן
אין דעם – אינעם
מיט דעם – מיטן
פֿאַר דעם – פֿאַרן
פֿון דעם – פֿונעם
צו דעם – צום

Sample sentence with the dative case

Here is an example of a sentence that contains the dative case with a preposition, with articles and adjectives:

דער שיינער מענטש לייענט דאָס גרויסע בוך וועגן דער שיינער שטאָט.

Translation:

The nice person reads/is reading the great book about the beautiful city.

verb = לייענט

subject of verb = nominative case: masculine, singular = דער שיינער מענטש

direct object (reads *what/whom*?) = accusative case, neuter, singular = דאָס גרויסע בוך

preposition = וועגן

dative case (governed by the preposition), feminine, singular = דער שיינער שטאָט

Here is an example of a sentence that contains the dative case with an indirect object, with articles and adjectives:

דער שיינער מענטש גיט דער גוטער מאַמע דאָס גרויסע בוך.

Translations:

The nice person gives/is giving the good mother the big book.
The nice person gives/is giving the big book **to** the good mother.

verb = גיט

subject of verb = nominative case, masculine, singular = דער שיינער מענטש

direct object (gives + *what/whom*?) = accusative case, neuter, singular = דאָס גרויסע בוך

indirect object (gives + *to/for whom*?) = dative case, feminine, singular = דער גוטער מאַמע

The above sentence could be formulated as follows with no change in meaning:

דער שיינער מענטש גיט דאָס גרויסע בוך דער גוטער מאַמע.

Note that the preposition remains implied despite the change in word order.

Idiomatic constructions with the dative case (dative of reference)

The dative case is used to form idiomatic constructions that express human experience (an experience that happens *to* someone).

Subjective feelings

The dative of reference is used to express feelings. These include feeling good or not good, or feeling happy.

In these cases, the adjective appears in the predicate and the verb agrees with an imaginary subject pronoun: "it עס." This "it" can fill the first position of a Yiddish sentence or be implied. It does not refer back to any actual subject, but behaves like the "it" in the English expression, "it is raining" and is known as an "expletive עס." When another sentence unit already occupies the first position, the "עס" is not used.

Examples:

Motl feels good.	עס איז מאָטלען גוט.
Motl feels good.	מאָטלען איז גוט.
Motl doesn't feel good.	עס איז מאָטלען ניט גוט.
Motl doesn't feel good.	מאָטלען איז ניט גוט.
Motl feels happy.	עס איז מאָטלען פֿריילעך.
Now Motl feels happy.	איצט איז מאָטלען פֿריילעך.

The verb to like *געפֿעלן*

The dative case is also used to form the verb *to like* געפֿעלן, which functions like the English verb "to appeal to."

The verb געפֿעלן

PERSON/THING THAT IS LIKED Nominative case	+	conjugated form of געפֿעלן	+	PERSON/THING THAT IS DOING THE LIKING Dative case
		or		
PERSON/THING THAT IS DOING THE LIKING Dative case	+	conjugated form of געפֿעלן	+	PERSON/THING THAT IS LIKED Nominative case

Like all verbs, געפֿעלן will agree with the subject, which is the verb in the nominative case.

Examples:

Motl likes the books (i.e. the books appeal to Motl).

די ביכער געפֿעלן מאָטלען.
מאָטלען געפֿעלן די ביכער.
עס געפֿעלן מאָטלען די ביכער.
עס געפֿעלן די ביכער מאָטלען.

Note that all of these Yiddish sentences have the same English meaning: what differs is the word order and the presence of the "expletive עס."

Declension of nouns

Except for singular versus plural, nouns do not inflect in Yiddish.

Here are the very few exceptions to this rule, generally referring to words for people that function almost in the capacity of proper names.

1. A short list of masculine nouns inflect like proper names in the accusative and dative cases.

Translation	Accusative-Dative	Nominative
the father	דעם טאַטן	דער טאַטע
the grandfather	דעם זיידן	דער זיידע
the Jew	דעם ייִדן	דער ייִד
the person	דעם מענטשן	דער מענטש
the rabbi	דעם רבין	דער רבי

2. The following feminine nouns inflect in the dative case (and in some cases in the accusative):

Translation	Dative	Nominative
the grandmother	דער באָבען	די באָבע
the mother	דער מאַמען	די מאַמע
the aunt	דער מומען	די מומע

The dative as possessive case

Yiddish does not have a separate possessive (genitive) case. The possessive is generally indicated by use of possessive pronouns and endings on proper names.

In order to indicate possession by a named person, a ס is added to the end of the name.

An ending of עס is added in the possessive if the name ends in the following letters: דזש, דז, ז, טש, ש, ץ, ס. There is no apostrophe unless the name already ends in ס.

The noun being possessed retains the same case as it would with a possessive pronoun or indefinite article.

Examples:

Motl's book is nice. — מאָטלס בוך איז שיין.
I have Rabinovitch's book — איך האָב ראַבינאָוויטשעס בוך.
One is talking about Weiss's book. — מען רעדט וועגן ווייס' בוך.

Nouns or noun phrases in the possessive appear in the dative case followed by an ending of ס (or עס). The noun or noun phrase doing the possessing appears in the dative case (governed by an imaginary "of"). *Note that the noun being possessed retains its original case. This is a relatively rare construction in Yiddish.

Examples:

The beautiful city's book is great.
I.e. the book of the beautiful city.
*בוך is nominative

דער שיינער שטאָטס בוך איז גרויס.

I love the mother's book.
I.e. the book of the mother.
*בוך is accusative

איך האָב ליב **דער מאַמענס** בוך.

One is talking about the person's book.
I.e. the book of the person.
*בוך is dative (it follows a preposition)

מען רעדט וועגן **דעם מענטשנס** בוך.

Summary: case table and guide

Dative *prepositions/indirect object*	Accusative *direct object*	Nominative *subject*	Gender/number
דעם –ן אַ –ן	דעם –ן אַ –ן	דער –ער אַ –ער	Masculine
דער –ער אַ –ער	די –ע אַ –ע	די –ע אַ –ע	Feminine
דעם –ן	דאָס –ע	דאָס –ע	Neuter definite
אַ –	אַ –	אַ –	Neuter indefinite
די –ע –ע	די –ע –ע	די –ע –ע	Plural

Guide: determining the case of an article/adjective/noun

1. Locate the verb. Note: This should be the inflected (conjugated) verb.
2. Locate the subject of the verb: who is *verb*-ing?
   The subject of the inflected verb is in the nominative case.
   Reminder: The verb and its doer will always agree in person and number.
3. Locate the direct object, if any: verb + *what/whom*?
   The direct object of the verb is in the accusative case.
4. Find any prepositions: preposition + *what/whom*?
   The direct object of a preposition is in the dative case.
5. Find any indirect objects where the preposition "to" or "for" is implied: verb + *to/for what/whom*?
   The indirect object of the verb is in the dative case.
   Note: A Yiddish sentence will not necessarily contain all of the cases.

   Here is a sentence containing all of the Yiddish cases:

   דער גוטער מענטש לייענט דער שיינער מאַמען דאָס גרויסע בוך אין דער קליינער שטאָט.

1. What is the conjugated verb?
   Answer: לייענט.
   What do we know about לייענט?
   Answer: the ט ending on the verb indicates that it is third person singular or second person plural (possible subjects: any singular noun, איר).
2. Who is doing the verb: who is reading?
   Answer: דער גוטער מענטש.
   What do we know about דער גוטער מענטש?
   Answer: it is masculine, plural and nominative. It agrees with the verb לייענט.
   We know this because of the S-V-O (subject-verb-object) tendency of Yiddish word order as well as the fact that the subject agrees with the verb in gender and number.
   In this case, the form דער גוטער מענטש can only appear in the nominative. This is because as a masculine, singular noun, it takes on the form דעם גוטן מענטשן in the accusative and dative cases.
3. Verb + *what/whom*: the good person is saying/telling + what/whom (not **to** whom).
   Answer: דאָס גרויסע בוך.
   What do we know about דאָס גרויסע בוך?
   Answer: it is neuter, singular, and accusative.
4. Are there any prepositions?
   Answer: אין
   Preposition + *what/whom?*
   Answer: דער קליינער שטאָט

What do we know about דער קליינער שטאָט?
Answer: it is feminine, singular and dative.
5) Verb + implied "*to/for what / to/for whom*?"
Answer: דער שיינער מאַמען.
What do we know about דער שיינער מאַמען?
Answer: it is feminine, singular and dative.
The English translations of the sentence would be:
- The great person reads/is reading the nice mother the great book in the small city.
- The great person reads/is reading the great book to the nice mother in the small city.

Exercise 13.1

Provide the gender and number of each noun phrase provided here in the nominative case. Then provide the accusative and dative forms.

1. דער גרויסער מענטש*
2. אַ גרויסע שטאָט
3. דאָס שיינע בוך
4. פֿריילעכע מענטשן
5. אַ גוט בוך
6. קליינע מאַמעס
7. אַ שיינער קלאַס
8. די פֿריילעכע חתונה
9. די גוטע מאַמעס
10. אַ גוטער מענטש*

Reminder: the word מענטש is one of a short list of nouns that inflects in the accusative and dative cases to מענטשן. Despite the change in form, it remains singular in number. Compare with #4 above, where it is in the plural. This is clear because of the plural ending on the adjective in the noun phrase.

Exercise 13.2

Each sentence contains a preposition followed by a noun phrase in the nominative case in {}. Change the form of the noun phrase (article/adjective/noun) that follows a preposition into the dative form. Use contracted forms of the prepositions whenever possible.

Example: מיטן = מיט דעם

1. מיר שלאָפֿן בײַ {דער גוטער מענטש}.
2. איך ווייס וועגן {די שיינע היים}.
3. מען עסט מיט {דער גרויסער קלאַס}.
4. זיי פֿאָרן אויף {די גרויסע חתונה}.
5. איר זײַט פֿון {די קליינע שטאָט}.

Exercise 13.3

Translate the sentences in 13.2 into English.

Exercise 13.4

Break down the sentences into their component parts. Here is one suggested notation (different colours are also a good option):

1) **Verb**
2) <u>Nominatives</u> (any articles/adjectives/nouns or pronouns)
3) <u>Accusatives</u> (any articles/adjectives/nouns or pronouns)
4) *Prepositions*
5) Datives (any articles/adjectives/nouns or pronouns)

Reminders: Not every sentence will have an accusative and a dative; some may have more than one. The word order is not necessarily S-V-O.

1. אַלע מענטשן זײַנען אין דעם גרויסן קלאַס.
2. זיי לייענען דאָס גוטע בוך וועגן אַ שיינער שטאָט בײַ דער מאַמען.
3. עס איז מאָטלען גוט אויף דער חתונה און די מענטשן געפֿעלן דער מאַמען.
4. זי פֿאָרט קיין ניו–יאָרק מיט דער מאַמען.
5. איך גיב דעם גוטן מענטשן דער מאַמענס בוך.

Exercise 13.5

Translate each of the sentences in exercise 13.4 into English.

UNIT 14

Declension of pronouns

In Yiddish, pronouns decline in the same three grammatical cases as nouns: nominative, accusative and dative. All pronouns that are subjects of conjugated verbs (doers of the action) are in the nominative case. When a pronoun is not the subject of the verb, it appears in a different forms: a pronoun as the direct object appears in the accusative case, and a pronoun that is governed by a preposition or an indirect object appears in the dative case.

Declension of pronouns

(this is not an exhaustive list)

Dative	Accusative	Nominative	Person
מיר	מיך	איך	First person singular
דיר	דיך	דו	Second person singular
אים	אים	ער	Third person singular masculine
איר	זי	זי	Third person singular feminine
אים	עס	עס	Third person singular neuter
Exists only in the nominative		מען	Third person singular impersonal
אונדז	אונדז	מיר	First person plural
אײַך	אײַך	איר	Second person plural
זיי	זיי	זיי	Third person plural
וואָס	וואָס	וואָס	"what"
וועמען	וועמען	ווער	"who"
עמעצן	עמעצן	עמעצער	"someone"
קיינעם	קיינעם	קיינער	"no one"
גאָרניט	גאָרניט	גאָרניט	"nothing"

Note that the pronouns that refer to a general group of people (someone, no one) appear in the masculine.

The pronoun *every, each* יעדער has two formulations:

1. As a pronoun that replaces a noun/nouns, it inflects according to gender and case, with no neuter.

Declension of יעדער

Dative	Accusative	Nominative	
יעדערן	יעדערן	יעדערער	Masculine
יעדערער	יעדערע	יעדערע	Feminine

The masculine form is used for groups of men and women.

Examples:

Everyone goes/is going to the park. יעדערער גייט אין פּאַרק.
She loves everyone. זי האָט יעדערן ליב.

The neuter form, יעדעס, is also found.

2. When used before a noun, יעדער does not inflect.

Example:

He reads every book. ער לייענט יעדער בוך.

Examples of sentences with pronouns in all declensions:

You go with **me**. **דו** גייסט מיט **מיר**.
You go with **us**. **דו** גייסט מיט **אונדז**.
I know about **him**. **איך** ווייס וועגן **אים**.
I know about **them**. **איך** ווייס וועגן **זיי**.
Who are **you**? **ווער** ביסטו?
Whom do **you** have? **וועמען** האָסטו?
Some one is writing (to) **her**. **עמעצער** שרײַבט **איר**.
No one is writing. **קיינער** שרײַבט ניט.

Third person pronouns can replace nouns provided they agree in gender, number and case.

Examples:

Translation	Pronoun	Form of noun	Sentence
The **person/he** is good.	**ער** איז גוט.	*masculine, singular, nominative*	**דער מענטש** איז גוט.
One eats with **the mother/her**.	מען עסט מיט **איר**.	*feminine, singular, dative*	מען עסט מיט **דער מאַמען**.
He reads **a book/it**.	ער לייענט **עס**.	*neuter, singular, accusative*	ער לייענט **אַ בוך**.
He reads **books/them**.	ער לייענט **זיי**.	*neuter, plural, accusative*	ער לייענט **ביכער**.

Exercise 14.1

Each sentence contains a personal pronoun in {} in the nominative case.

In each sentence, identify the person and number of the verb and the gender, number and case of all noun phrases or pronouns not in {}. Then determine as much information about the ________ {} as you can and provide the correct declined form of the personal pronoun (it may be nominative, accusative or dative).

Example:

גיב {איך}_______ דאָס בוך!

Verb: גיב. Second person imperative mood (!). This means that there will be no nominative (verbs that command do not have subjects).

Noun phrase: דאָס בוך. Neuter, singular, accusative (its form indicates that it is nominative or accusative but the verb in this sentence does not have a subject).

{איך} This pronoun is first person, singular. It will be in the dative case: give to what/to whom? The declined pronoun form is:

גיב מיר דאָס בוך!

1. די מאַמע טוט {עס}_______.
2. {ווער}_______ גיט דער מענטש דאָס בוך?
3. {יעדער}_______ פֿאָרט אין דער שיינער שטאָט.
4. איך גיי מיט {איר}_______.
5. דאָס בוך געפֿעלט {מיר}_______ ניט.

Exercise 14.2

Translate your answers from 14.1 into English.

Exercise 14.3

Replace each of the nouns in bold with the corresponding third person pronoun (match the gender, number and case).

1. **די מאַמע** עסט.
2. איך ווייס ניט ווער **דער מענטש** איז.
3. זיי האָבן **שיינע ביכער**.
4. אַלע מענטשן גייען מיט **דער מאַמען**.
5. ווער לייענט **דאָס בוך**?

Exercise 14.4

Translate your answers in 14.3 into English.

Exercise 14.5

Translate the following sentences into Yiddish.

1. He knows it very well.
2. Why is she giving him every book?
3. I am not doing it!
4. Who is their mother?
5. No one is traveling with you (plural).

UNIT 15

The pronoun זיך

The pronoun זיך can have several functions in Yiddish. As a pronoun, it does not decline but rather retains the same form for all persons, singular and plural. It can function as both an accusative or dative pronoun.

The uses of the pronoun זיך fall into different categories, including:

1. True reflexive: זיך used as the object or indirect object of a verb or of a preposition when the person it refers to is the same as the subject of the sentence.

   Example:

   He gives **himself** a book. ער גיט זיך אַ בוך.

   The adverb אַליין can be used in conjunction with זיך to underline the fact that the object is the same person as the subject.

   Example:

   He gives *himself* a book. ער גיט זיך אַליין אַ בוך.

2. As a verbal additive in reciprocal action: people doing an action to each other.

   Example:

   They give/are giving each other books. זיי געבן זיך ביכער.

3. As a verbal additive in inherently reflexive verbs: some verbs are formed with זיך as part of the verb. זיך forms part of the verb in all tenses.

Vocabulary: examples of inherently reflexive verbs

to learn, study	לערנען זיך
to play (without an object)	שפּילן זיך

Note the difference in the meaning of these verbs without the זיך:

to teach	לערנען
to play (requires an object)	שפּילן

Examples:

We are learning/studying Yiddish. מיר לערנען זיך ייִדיש.
He is teaching Yiddish. ער לערנט ייִדיש.
They play/are playing in the park. זיי שפּילן זיך אין פּאַרק.
She plays/is playing piano. זי שפּילט פּיאַנע.

4. As a verbal additive to indicate action performed in solitude.

Example:

He is walking along by himself. ער גייט זיך.

Exercise 15.1

Translate the following sentences into English, noting the different uses of the pronoun זיך.

1. די מענטשן שפּילן זיך.
2. ער גיט זיך אַליין אַ גוט בוך.
3. לערנט זיך ייִדיש!
4. די מענטשן גיבן זיך שיינע ביכער.
5. פֿאַרוואָס לערנט מען זיך ניט?

UNIT 16

Yiddish word order 3: verbs with more than one part: the periphrastic verb *to like, love* ליב האָבן

Verbs with more than one part

Yiddish has many verb formations with more than one part: the auxiliary (helping verb), which is inflected (i.e. it conjugates), and other non-inflected parts such as an invariable element, an infinitive, a past participle, or a adverbial complement.

The periphrastic verb *to like, love* ליב האָבן

One category of Yiddish verbs with more than one part is *periphrastic verbs*, which consist of an auxiliary verb that inflects/conjugates + an invariable/uninflected element. Yiddish has a large number of these verbs. They use the auxiliary verbs האָבן, זײַן, ווערן, and others. Many periphrastic verbs include an invariable element that stems from the *loshn-koydesh* (pre-Modern Hebrew-Aramaic) component of Yiddish.

Vocabulary: examples of periphrastic verbs

Note: These words do not form part of this text's working vocabulary.

Translation	Example of conjugation	Translation	*Loshn-koydesh* pronunciation	Infinitive
I marry	איך האָב חתונה	to marry	*khasene*	חתונה האָבן
I agree	איך בין מסכּים	To agree	*maskim*	מסכּים זײַן
I transform	איך ווער מגולגל	to transform	*megulgl*	מגולגל ווערן

The verb ליב האָבן translates in English as "to like" or "to love" (not "to *have* like/love").

The periphrastic verb *to like, love* ליב האָבן

Conjugation of ליב האָבן in the present indicative

Translation	Auxiliary: conjugated form		Invariable element	Person, number pronoun
I like/love	ליב	+	איך האָב	First person singular
You like/love			דו האָסט	Second person singular
He/she/it/one likes/loves			ער/זי/עס/ מען האָט	Third person singular
We like/love			מיר האָבן	First person plural
You like/love			איר האָט	Second person plural
They like/love			זיי האָבן	Third person plural

Example:

I like/love איך האָב ליב

The conjugation of the second person in the imperative mood is formed by adding the following endings to the base form of any Yiddish verb:

Translation	Invariable element		Auxiliary: conjugated form	Number
Like/love!	ליב!	+	האָב	singular, informal
Like/love!			האָט	plural/formal

Thus:

Like/love! האָב/האָט ליב!

How to use the verb ליב האָבן:

1. The verb ליב האָבן can take a direct object, which appears in the accusative case. This is how to express liking or loving + a person/place/thing.

   Example:

   I like/love **the big park**. איך האָב ליב **דעם גרויסן פּאַרק**.

2. The verb ליב האָבן can be followed by the particle צו and an infinitive of a verb. This is how to express liking or loving an activity.

   Example:

   I like/love **to write**. איך האָב ליב צו שרײַבן.

Note: The majority of Yiddish verbs do not require the particle צו when they are following an infinitive. The very few verbs that do require the particle צו before the infinitive include: *to begin* אָנהייבן (see Unit 20).

Word order 3

Rules of word order for verbs with more than one part

When a Yiddish verb contains more than one part, the inflected (conjugated part) appears in the second fixed position. The fixed (uninflected) part/invariable element appears in the third fixed position. As a rule, the two parts of the verb are not separated, if possible. However, all accusative and dative pronouns as well as the pronoun זיך must be positioned between them.

The negative particle ניט generally appears before the invariable element.

Note: See "Summary: basic rules of Yiddish word order" in Unit 8.

Examples:

Translations, notes	**4+**	**3**		**2/3**	**2**	**1**	**0**
	whatever remains	the un-inflected verb	ניט	direct object noun or pronoun, indirect object or pronoun, adverbs of time and place, subject noun or subject pronoun	the inflected verb*	any unit but the inflected verb*	nonunit words such as exclamations or conjunctions
					*Exceptions: "yes-no" questions and commands		

Translations, notes	**4+**	**3**		**2/3**	**2**	**1**	**0**
The mother has the book.				דאָס בוך.	האָט	די מאַמע	
However the mother does not have the book.	דאָס בוך.		ניט		האָט	די מאַמע	אָבער
The mother does not have it (the pronoun עס replaces דאָס בוך).			ניט.	עס	האָט	די מאַמע	
The mother likes/loves the book.	דאָס בוך.	ליב			האָט	די מאַמע	
The mother likes/loves *the book*.		ליב.		דאָס בוך	האָט	די מאַמע	
However the mother does not like/love the book.	דאָס בוך.	ליב	ניט		האָט	די מאַמע	אָבער
The mother does not like/love it.		ליב.	ניט	עס	האָט	די מאַמע	
The mother likes/loves herself.		ליב.		זיך	האָט	די מאַמע	
Does mother have the book?				דאָס בוך?	די מאַמע	האָט	
Does mother have the book?	דאָס בוך.	ליב			די מאַמע	האָט	

Exercise 16.1

Using the sentence units provided in the table below, construct Yiddish sentences. Make sure that your inflected verb is in the second position. Then translate the sentences into English.

Note: Q.5 is a question.

Examples:

Uninflected verb	Inflected verb	Accusative *object*	Nominative *subject*	
ליב	האָט	דעם פּאַרק	די מאַמע	*
ליב	האָט	אים	זי	**

The mother likes/loves the park. *די מאַמע האָט ליב דעם פּאַרק.**

She likes/loves it. *זי האָט אים ליב.***

Uninflected verb	Inflected verb	Accusative *object*	Nominative *subject*	
ליב	האָט	דאָס בוך	דער מענטש	1
		עס	ער	2
	האָבן	די מאַמע	מיר	3
		זי		4
	האָט	וועמען	איר	?5

Exercise 16.2

Negate your five sentences from 16.1. Then translate them into English.

Exercise 16.3

Translate the following sentences into Yiddish using the construction:

infinitive of verb + צו + ליב האָבן

Example:

He likes to write. .ער האָט ליב צו שרײַבן

1. She does not like to sleep.
2. We love to eat.
3. They like to read in (the) park.
4. I love to be here.
5. Do all people love to read?

Exercise 16.4

Identify the verb and nouns/pronouns in the nominative/accusative/dative cases in the English sentences and provide information about the gender, number, and case they will have in Yiddish translation. Then translate the sentences into Yiddish. Note: All of these sentences in this exercise employ S-V-O (subject-verb-object) word order.

Example:

He likes me.
Nominative: he (third person singular): ער
Verb: likes (third person singular): האָט ליב
Accusative: me (first person singular): מיך
Yiddish: .ער האָט מיך ליב

1. We love her!
2. People like to play with us.
3. Give (plural) me the book!
4. I am not reading it (the book).
5. Who is writing them (the books) in Yiddish?

UNIT 17

Mood: modal verbs, conjugations of the first and third person of the imperative mood, the subjunctive mood

Mood

Like the imperative mood already discussed in a previous chapter, all of the verb forms in this unit function to express attitudes towards actions that are unreal or contingent. They do not take place in real time and as a result have no tense.

Examples:

She wants to go home. We should have a nap. They must pay their bills. Let's go! Let them eat cake! I want you to go.

Modal verbs

Modal verbs are a group of verbs in Yiddish that act as auxiliary verbs for other verbs. They function to express actions that are not actually taking place but are possible, necessary, desired or permitted/not permitted. They convey a variety of different verbal moods in Yiddish.

The Yiddish modal verbs

Translation	Mood	Notes	Yiddish infinitive
to need, have to	necessitative		דאַרפֿן
to want to		stem = וויל	ווערלן
to ought, to should	necessitative		זאָלן
to be forbidden from	prohibitive	infinitive + ניט + טאָרן	טאָרן ניט

Translation	Mood	Notes	Yiddish infinitive
to must	obligative		מוזן
to be allowed to, may	permissive		מעגן
to know how, be able to			קענען

Modal verbs behave differently from other verbs in the present indicative in the following ways:

1. Modal verbs in the third person singular are formed by the base + *no ending* (like the first person singular).
2. Modal verbs are followed directly by the infinitive (no **צו**).

Examples:

She **needs/has to** know why. — זי **דאַרף** וויסן פֿאַרוואָס.
We **want to** eat. — מיר **ווילן** עסן.
You ought to/should go/travel home. — איר **זאָלט** פֿאָרן אַהיים.
You **must** sleep. — איר **מוזט** שלאָפֿן.
You **may** play. — דו **מעגסט** שפּילן זיך.
One **is forbidden to** write. — מען **טאָר ניט** שרײַבן.
He **knows how to/is able to** read. — ער **קען** לייענען.

Note: Some of the modal verbs also behave as regular verbs: that is, they can appear without infinitives and take direct objects. However, they always conjugate the same way.

Translation	Yiddish infinitive
to need (something)	דאַרפֿן
to want (something)	וועלן
to know (a language, a person)	קענען

Examples

We want the book. — מיר דאַרפֿן דאָס בוך.
You want the dog. — דו ווילסט דעם הונט.
He knows Yiddish. — ער קען ייִדיש.
He knows your mother. — ער קען דײַן מאַמע.

Conjugations of the first and third person of the imperative mood (the optative mood)

Unlike the second person of the imperative mood, which is formed by adding endings onto the base of the verb, the imperative mood conjugations for the first and third person are formed with an auxiliary and the infinitive of the verb.

First and third person conjugations of the imperative mood function as exhortations. They are much less direct than commands: one can only directly command a "you"; all other commands are incitements or encouragements.

First person conjugation of the imperative mood (optative mood)

		Auxiliary	Person
Infinitive of verb	+	לאָמיך	singular
		לאָמיר	plural

Examples:

Let me eat! לאָמיך עסן!
Let's eat! לאָמיר עסן!

Third person conjugation of the imperative mood

		Auxiliary	Person
Infinitive of verb	+	זאָל ער/זי/עס/מען	singular
		זאָלן זיי	plural

Examples:

Let him/her/it/one eat! זאָל ער/זי/עס/מען עסן!
Let them eat! זאָלן זיי עסן!

The verb זאָלן can also be used as a less direct alternative to the second person imperative.

Examples:

You should eat! דו זאָלסט עסן! / איר זאָלט עסן!

The subjunctive mood

The subjunctive is a verb form that expresses an action that is desired but hypothetical. Here is a formulation where the subjunctive functions as a less direct form of the imperative mood.

It is formed by joining two clauses as follows:

Infinitive of verb	Conjugated auxiliary זאָלן	Subject of verb זאָלן	Conjunction אַז or ,	Conjugated form of וועלן	Subject of verb וועלן

Examples:

I want you to go/travel.	איך וויל, דו זאָלסט פֿאָרן.
We want you to eat.	מיר ווילן אַז איר זאָלט עסן.
She wants them to sleep.	זי וויל אַז זיי זאָלן שלאָפֿן.

Exercise 17.1

Insert the correct form of the modal verb in front of the infinitive in each sentence. The modal verbs are provided in {}.

1. איך {זאָלן} _______ גיין אַהיים איצט.
2. מען {מוזן} _______ עסן גוט.
3. דו {טאָרן ניט} _______ שפּילן זיך דאָ.
4. אַלע מענטשן {דאַרפֿן} _______ שלאָפֿן.
5. די מאַמע {זאָלן} _______ זיך לערנען.
6. איר {מעגן} _______ שרײַבן.
7. זיי {קענען} _______ לייענען.

Exercise 17.2

Translate the sentences in 17.1 into English.

Exercise 17.3

Translate the following sentences into English.

1. איך וויל, דו זאָלסט עסן אַ ביסל.
2. זאָל ער לערנען זיך!
3. אַ מענטש מוז קענען ייִדיש.
4. איך וויל ניט אײַער בוך.
5. לאָמיך שלאָפֿן!

Exercise 17.4

Translate the following sentences into Yiddish.

1. Let me eat now!
2. She wants me to read this book.
3. I do not want to read it (the book).
4. Let them go/travel to the big city!
5. One knows that one needs to eat and sleep.

UNIT 18

The future tense

The future tense refers to a time following the utterance being made. The Yiddish future tense form corresponds to any of the following English constructions: I shall eat. I shall be eating.

The future tense form is comprised of an auxiliary verb plus the infinitive of a verb.

Note: The future auxiliary verb וועלן is defective: it exists in no other formulation in Yiddish, has no infinitive, and functions solely as a helping verb to form the future tense. The future auxiliary וועלן should not be confused with the verb *to want* וועלן in meaning or conjugation.

The future tense

Translation	Example: שלאָפֿן	Infinitive of verb	+	Auxiliary verb וועלן	Person, number
I shall sleep	איך וועל שלאָפֿן			איך וועל	First person singular
You will sleep	דו וועסט שלאָפֿן			דו וועסט	Second person singular
He will sleep	ער וועט שלאָפֿן			ער/זי/עס/ מען וועט	Third person singular
We shall sleep	מיר וועלן שלאָפֿן			מיר וועלן	First person plural
You will sleep	איר וועט שלאָפֿן			איר וועט	Second person plural
They will sleep	זיי וועלן שלאָפֿן			זיי וועלן	Third person plural

Note: Like modal verbs, there is no particle צו before the infinitive in the formation of the future tense.

Yiddish forms the immediate future tense by using the present tense conjugation of the verb גיין as auxiliary instead of וועלן. This indicates that the action is going to take place in the near rather than distant future.

Example:

I am going to read. איך גיי לייענען.

Exercise 18.1

Fill in the correct conjugation of the auxiliary verb וועלן to form the future tense in each number.

1. דו ______ שלאָפֿן
2. די מענטשן ______ לייענען
3. זי ______ האָבן
4. איך ______ טאָן
5. מען ______ געבן
6. מיר ______ זײַן
7. ______ איר עסן?

Exercise 18.2

The sentences below are in the present tense and need to be rewritten in the future tense. Verbs are highlighted in **bold**.

Reminder: If there are direct or indirect object pronouns or the negative particle ניט, they must appear between the inflected and fixed parts of the verb.

Note: Sentences with modal verbs (which already have two parts) will have three verbal parts.

Examples:

איך לייען דאָס בוך. איך וועל לייענען דאָס בוך.

איך לייען עס. איך וועל עס לייענען. *personal pronoun*

איך לייען ניט דאָס בוך. איך וועל ניט לייענען דאָס בוך. *negative*

איך קען לייענען דאָס בוך. איך וועל קענען לייענען דאָס בוך. *modal verb*

1. זיי **גייען** אין קלאַס.
2. ווער **עסט** בײַ אונדז?
3. מען **גיט** דער מאַמען אַ בוך.
4. איך **טו** עס ניט.
5. דו **ווילסט שרײַבן**.

Exercise 18.3

Translate the sentences in 18.2 into English, both the present tense versions and your answers (future tense formulations).

Examples (from 18.2):

I read the book. I shall read the book.
I read it. I shall read it.
I do not read/am not reading the book. I shall not read the book.
I can/am able to read the book. I shall be able to read the book.

UNIT 19
The past tense

The past tense

The past tense refers to a time preceding the utterance being made. Yiddish has one primary way of forming the past tense to convey the following meanings:

I slept. I was sleeping. I had been sleeping.

Repeated action in the past ("I used to sleep") has its own construction, which is discussed in Unit 21.

The past tense is formed with an auxiliary verb and a past participle. Like the auxiliary verb װעלן in the future tense, the auxiliary verb in the past serves as a helping verb to indicate that the action has taken place in the past.

All Yiddish verbs fall into two major categories:

1. Most verbs use the verb האָבן as their auxiliary. All "transitive verbs" use the auxiliary האָבן. Transitive verbs are verbs that can take a direct object.
   For example: one can eat, read, know, love + *something/someone.*
2. A smaller group of verbs use the verb זײַן as their auxiliary. All of these are "intransitive verbs." Intransitive verbs cannot take a direct object.
   For example: one cannot travel, jump, travel + *something/someone*.

A list of the past participles in this category is found below.

Note: Not all intransitive verbs automatically conjugate with זײַן as the auxiliary. However, all transitive verbs conjugate with האָבן.

Past participles fall into three main categories:

1. Most Yiddish verbs fall into a category of "weak verbs" whose participles are formed as follows:

ט + base of verb + גע

Reminder: The base of a verb infinitive is the infinitive minus the ending of ען or ן.

Examples:

לייענען – גע + לייענ + ט = געלייענט
שפּילן – גע + שפּיל + ט = געשפּילט

2. Other verbs fall into the category of "strong verbs" and are formed as follows:

ן + base of verb, often with vowel changes + **גע**

However, there is no way to determine a priori whether a Yiddish infinitive is "weak" or "strong." Yiddish past participles are thus best memorized.

3. Verbs whose first syllables do not bear primary stress (as is the normal pattern in Yiddish) do not take the prefix –גע. These include inseparable prefix verbs (discussed in Unit 20) and verbs with the suffix –ירן such as קאָריגירן (past participle: קאָריגירט).

A general guide to forming the past tense

Note: Although the chart offers only one translation, every verb in the Yiddish past tense can be translated to express different shades of meaning.

Examples:

I gave, I was giving, I have given — איך האָב געגעבן
I read, I was reading, I have read — איך האָב געלייענט
I wrote, I was writing, I have written — איך האָב געשריבן

Translation Example in first person singular	Examples infinitive: past tense form	Form of past participle	+	Conjugated auxiliary verbs
To read: I read	לייענען: איך האָב געלייענט	ט– base of verb –גע		האָבן Auxiliary for most verbs. Auxiliary for "transitive verbs"
To give: I gave To do: I did	געבן: איך האָב געגעבן טאָן: איך האָב געטאָן	ן– base of verb –גע		

Translation Example in first person singular	Examples infinitive: past tense form	Form of past participle	+	Conjugated auxiliary verbs
To know: I knew	װיסן: איך האָב געװוּסט	ט– modified base –גע		
To wrote: I wrote	שרײַבן: איך האָב געשריבן	ן– modified base –גע		
To have: I had To eat: I ate	האָבן: איך האָב געהאַט עסן: איך האָב געגעסן	Irregular forms		
To travel: I traveled	פֿאָרן: איך בין געפֿאָרן	ן– base of verb –גע		זײַן Auxiliary for a small group of "intransitive verbs"
To become: I became	װערן: איך בין געװאָרן	ן– modified base –גע		
To be: I was To go: I went	זײַן: איך בין געװען גײן: איך בין געגאַנגען	Irregular forms		

Past tense of modal verbs

Most modal verbs follow the pattern for "weak verbs" in past tense construction. That is, they use האָבן as the auxiliary verb and the ט + *base of verb* + גע pattern for their past participles.

Thus:

Translation	Past tense	Modal verb infinitive
I had to	איך האָב געדאַרפֿט	דאַרפֿן
I ought to have, I should have	איך האָב געזאָלט	זאָלן
I had to	איך האָב געמוזט	מוזן
I was allowed to	איך האָב געמעגט	מעגן
I was forbidden from	איך האָב ניט געטאָרט	טאָרן ניט
I knew how to, was able to	איך האָב געקענט	קענען

There is one exception (note the vowel change in the form of the base):

I wanted to איך האָב געוואָלט וועלן

Intransitive verbs that conjugate with זייַן as auxiliary

Note: The new verbs on this list do not form part of this text's working vocabulary.

Translation	Past participle	Infinitive
remained	געבליבן	בלייַבן
went (on foot)	געגאַנגען	גיין
liked (see Unit 13)	געפֿעלן	געפֿעלן
hung*	געהאָנגען	הענגען
grew*	געוואָקסן	וואַקסן
became	געוואָרן	ווערן
was	געווען	זייַן
sat	געזעסן	זיצן
ran	געלאָפֿן	לויפֿן
lay	געלעגן	ליגן
fell	געפֿאַלן	פֿאַלן
traveled (not on foot)	געפֿאָרן	פֿאָרן
flew	געפֿלויגן	פֿליען
came	געקומען	קומען
crawled	געקראָכן	קריכן
died	געשטאָרבן	שטאַרבן
stood	געשטאַנען	שטיין
slept	געשלאָפֿן	שלאָפֿן
jumped	געשפּרונגען	שפּרינגען

Reminder: These verbs cannot take a direct object.

The verbs marked with * above can be both transitive and intransitive.

Note the difference:

Intransitive form		
No direct object Example: I **hung** (from a tree).	איך בין געהאָנגען	הענגען
No direct object Example: I **grew** (bigger).	איך בין געוואָקסן	וואַקסן
Transitive form		
Direct object Example: I **hung** *something (e.g. a picture).*	איך האָב געהאָנגען	הענגען
Direct object Example: I **grew** *something (e.g. vegetables).*	איך האָב געוואָקסן	וואַקסן

The pluperfect tense (I had eaten איך האָב געהאַט געגעסן) and future past tense (I will have eaten איך וועל האָבן געגעסן) are rarely used in Yiddish.

Exercise 19.1

Provide the correct auxiliary verb and past participle for each of the following verbs in the past tense. Then conjugate each verb.

Verbs indicated by * follow the pattern for "weak verbs." That is, they use האָבן as the auxiliary verb and the ט + *base of verb* + גע pattern for the past participles.

The others are "strong verbs" that either use זײַן as the auxiliary or have an irregular past participle, such as a vowel change. These should be memorized as they are encountered.

Examples:

*דאַרפֿן: האָבן + געדאַרפֿט
איך האָב געדאַרפֿט, דו האָסט געדאַרפֿט, ער/זי/עס/מען האָט געדאַרפֿט,
מיר האָבן געדאַרפֿט, איר האָט געדאַרפֿט, זיי האָבן געדאַרפֿט
ווערן: זײַן + געוואָרן
איך בין געוואָרן, דו ביסט געוואָרן, ער/זי/עס/מען איז געוואָרן,
מיר זײַנען געוואָרן, איר זײַט געוואָרן, זיי זײַנען געוואָרן

1. האָבן
2. *לייענען
3. זײַן
4. טאָן
5. געבן

6. גיין
7. *לערנען
8. פֿאָרן
9. *שפּילן
10. *קענען

Exercise 19.2

In each sentence, provide the correct form of the auxiliary and past participle for each infinitive provided in {}. Then translate each sentence into English.

Example:

איך *{גיין}*_______ _______ אין קלאַס.

איך בין געגאַנגען אין קלאַס. *I went to class.*

1. אַלע מענטשן {וועלן}_______ _______ דאָס בוך.
2. זיי {שפּילן}_______ _______ מיט אונדז.
3. מען {עסן}_______ _______ אַ ביסל.
4. ווער {לערנען זיך}_______ _______ דאָ?
5. די מאַמע {זײַן}_______ _______ פֿריילעך.

Exercise 19.3

The sentences below are in the present tense and need to be rewritten in the past tense. Verbs are highlighted in **bold**.

Reminder: If there are direct or indirect object pronouns or the negative particle **ניט**, they must appear between the inflected and fixed parts of the verb.

Note: Sentences with modal verbs (which already have two parts) will have three verbal parts.

Examples:

איך **לייען** דאָס בוך. *איך **האָב** **געלייענט** דאָס בוך.*

איך **לייען עס**. *איך **האָב** עס **געלייענט**.* personal pronoun

איך **לייען ניט** דאָס בוך. *איך **האָב** ניט **געלייענט** דאָס בוך.* negative

איך **קען לייענען** דאָס בוך. *איך **האָב** **געקענט לייענען** דאָס בוך.* modal verb

1. זיי **גייען** אין קלאַס.
2. ווער **עסט** בײַ אונדז?
3. מען **גיט** דער מאַמען אַ בוך.
4. איך **טו** עס ניט.
5. דו **ווילסט שרײַבן**.

Exercise 19.4

Translate the following sentences into Yiddish paying special attention to word order.

1. She really wanted to become a happy person.
2. We did not like his book so we did not read it.

   Reminder: In a declarative statement there is no word for the concept of "so" in the sense of "therefore": it is achieved through word order by placing the conjugated verb or part of the verb in the second position.

3. I gave you (plural) my book so read it (plural)!

   Reminder: In the case of imperatives, the word for "so" in the sense of "therefore" is the conjunction טאָ.

4. Whose mother went to the wedding in the big city?
5. We ate very well and we slept a little.

UNIT 20

Verbs with prefixes: separable prefix verbs (complemented verbs), inseparable prefix verbs

Verbs with prefixes

Verbs with prefixes abound in Yiddish. They behave like other, non-prefixed verbs: they have infinitives, and they conjugate in various tenses and moods.

Many verbs with prefixes fall loosely into the category of aspect. That is, they indicate something about the manner in which an action takes place, in particular whether it is perfective (a completed action).

Examples of prefixed verbs:

Translation	Present tense conjugation	Prefixed verb
I set down (in writing)	איך שרײַב אָן	אָנשרײַבן
I record (in writing) I register (e.g. for a class)	איך פֿאַרשרײַב איך פֿאַרשרײַב זיך	פֿאַרשרײַבן פֿאַרשרײַבן זיך

(Note: These examples are not part of this text's working vocabulary.)

The first example indicates completeness of action (I wrote it down). The second has a very specific set of meanings that are provided by the prefix.

Prefixed verbs are one of the most challenging areas of Yiddish grammar. While sometimes the meaning of verbs with prefixes can be deduced from the meaning of the verb and the general meaning of the prefix, they should be considered as new vocabulary words (and are listed in dictionaries accordingly).

Separable prefix verbs (complemented verbs)

Separable prefix verbs, or complemented verbs, are composed of two parts: a verb and a stressed prefix in the form of an adverbial complement.

Adverbial complements include:

אויס–, אויפֿ–, אומ–, אונטער–, איבער–, אײַנ–, אָנ–, אָפּ–, בײַ–, פֿאָר–, צו–.

The adverbial complement changes the meaning of the verb, either by adding a characteristic, such as completeness or suddenness of action, or by creating a new meaning entirely.

Note: A full discussion of this topic is beyond the scope of this text.

Vocabulary: examples of complemented verbs

Translation	Verb	Adverbial complement	Infinitive of verb
to get up/stand up **meaning of* שטיין*: to stand*	שטיין	־אויפֿ	אויפֿשטיין
to begin **meaning of* הייבן*: to lift*	הייבן	־אָנ	אָנהייבן

The adverbial complement is stressed in pronunciation. This is why the prefix separates from the rest of the verb in certain cases (e.g. the present tense).

The stress is indicated in **bold**: **אויפֿ**שטיין, **אָנ**הייבן

Conjugation of complemented verbs

Present indicative tense and second person conjugation of the imperative mood

In the present indicative tense and second person conjugation of the imperative mood, the adverbial complement separates from the verbal component.

Conjugation of complemented verbs in the present indicative

Translation	Adverbial complement	+	Present tense conjugation of verb	
I get/stand up	אויף		איך שטיי	Example 1
I begin	אָן		איך הייב	Example 2

Conjugation of complemented verbs in the second person of the imperative mood

Translation	Examples			Conjugation	
Get/stand up! Start!	!שטיי אויף !הייב אָן	adverbial complement	+	base of verb	singular, informal
Get/stand up! Start!	!שטייט אויף !הייבט אָן			ט + base of verb	plural/ formal

The rules concerning word order are the same for all verbs with two parts: an inflected and uninflected part (in this case, the adverbial complement).

Examples:

I start/am starting the book. איך הייב אָן דאָס בוך.
I do not start/am not starting the book. איך הייב ניט אָן דאָס בוך.
I start/am starting it. איך הייב עס אָן.
I start/am not starting it. איך הייב עס ניט אָן.

Infinitive + צו

The particle צו that is required before the infinitive in some constructions appears after the adverbial complement with no spaces before or after:

אויפֿ + צו + שטיין = אויפֿצושטיין

Example:

I like/love to get up/stand up. איך האָב ליב אויפֿצושטיין.

Reminder: The form of the infinitive with צו appears with only a few verbs such as "to like/love." Modal verbs and the future tense are simply followed by the infinitive.

Thus:

I want to get up/stand up. איך וויל אויפֿשטיין.

Conjugation of complemented verbs in other tenses

Except for the present indicative and second person conjugation of the imperative mood, adverbial complements do not separate from the verb.

Future tense conjugation of complemented verbs

The future tense of complemented verbs is formed identically to non-complemented verbs: the auxiliary וועלן + the infinitive.

Translation	Example	Infinitive		Auxiliary verb	Complemented verb
I shall get up	איך וועל אויפֿשטיין	אויפֿשטיין	+	וועלן	אויפֿשטיין
I shall begin	איך וועל אָנהייבן	אָנהייבן			אָנהייבן

Examples:

I shall start the book. — .איך וועל אָנהייבן דאָס בוך
I shall not start the book. — .איך וועל ניט אָנהייבן דאָס בוך
I shall start it. — .איך וועל עס אָנהייבן

Past tense conjugation of complemented verbs

The past tense of complemented verbs is formed like other verbs: the auxiliary verb (האָבן or זײַן) + a past participle. The same rules (transitive/intransitive) apply for determining the auxiliary verb.

The past participle is formed by the adverbial complement, followed by the גע (if there is one) and rest of the verb.

Note: Complemented verbs that have a counterpart without an adverbial complement will share the same auxiliary and past participle (minus the adverbial complement).

Thus:

Translation	Example	Past participle	Auxiliary verb	Complemented verb
I got up/was getting up	איך בין אויפֿגעשטאַנען	אויפֿגעשטאַנען *שטיין: געשטאַנען*	זײַן	אויפֿשטיין
I began/was beginning	איך האָב אָנגעהויבן	אָנגעהויבן *הייבן: געהויבן*	האָבן	אָנהייבן

Examples:

I started/was starting the book. איך האָב אָנגעהויבן דאָס בוך.
I did not start/was not starting the book. איך האָב ניט אָנגעהויבן דאָס בוך.
I started/was starting it. איך האָב עס אָנגעהויבן.

Note: אָנהייבן is one of a few verbs, like ליב האָבן, which are followed by the particle צו before the infinitive.

Example:

I am starting to read the book. איך הייב אָן **צו** לייענען דאָס בוך.
I shall start to read the book. איך וועל אָנהייבן **צו** לייענען דאָס בוך.
I started to read the book. איך האָב אָנגעהויבן **צו** לייענען דאָס בוך.

Summary of conjugations and other constructions using complemented verbs

אָנהייבן	אויפֿשטיין	Infinitive
איך הייב אָן	איך שטיי אויף	Present indicative
הייב/הייבט אָן!	שטיי/שטייט אויף!	Second person imperative
אָנצוהייבן	אויפֿצושטיין	Infinitive + צו
אָנגעהויבן	אויפֿגעשטאַנען	Past participle
איך האָב אָנגעהויבן	איך בין אויפֿגעשטאַנען	Past tense
איך וועל אָנהייבן	איך וועל אויפֿשטיין	Future tense

Free stressed prefixes

Yiddish has a sizeable group of prefixes that can be attached to verbs as needed.

For example:

Translation	Example	General meaning	Unstressed prefix
to leave	אַוועקגיין	away	אַוועק–

Unstressed prefixes can also appear without the main verb when it is implied, in particular with verbs of motion such as גיין.

For example:

Translation	Sample sentence	Infinitive
I left/went away.	.(איך בין אַוועק (איך בין אַוועקגעגאַנגען	אַוועקגיין

Inseparable prefix verbs

Yiddish has a sizeable group of verbs with inseparable prefixes. These prefixes, which are unstressed, never separate from the rest of the verb.

Inseparable prefix verbs fall into six categories. Some of the prefixes share general tendencies in the meaning of the verbs. (For example, some of the prefixes can serve to render an action perfective, that is, complete rather than in progress.) Examples of verbs in each category of general tendencies are indicated by *.

Vocabulary: examples of inseparable prefix verbs

Note: In addition to the verb *to like* געפֿעלן (see Unit 13) only the verb *to understand* פֿאַרשטיין forms part of this text's working vocabulary.

General tendencies *not for all verbs*	Translation	Example	Prefix
movement away from, undoing	to run away	אַנטלויפֿן*	אַנט-
creation of a state of existence	to decide	באַשליסן	באַ-
most verb stems do not exist without the prefix	to remember to like (to appeal to)	געדענקען געפֿעלן*	גע-
perfective: completeness of action to its conclusion	to tell, recount to shoot (dead)	דערציילן דערשיסן*	דער-
completeness of action; something done with negative outcome	to understand to sell to misplay, lose	פֿאַרשטיין פֿאַרקויפֿן* פֿאַרשפּילן*	פֿאַר-
explosive action, moving apart	to break	צעברעכן*	צע-

Note: A full discussion of this topic is beyond the scope of this text.

Conjugation of inseparable prefix verbs

The conjugation of these verbs in the present indicative, the second person of the imperative mood, and in the infinitive form with auxiliary verbs is identical to verbs without inseparable prefixes.

Future tense	Present tense second person imperative	Verb
איך וועל אַנטלויפֿן	איך אַנטלויף אַנטלויף! אַנטלויפֿט!	אַנטלויפֿן
איך וועל באַשליסן	איך באַשליס באַשליס! באַשליסט!	באַשליסן
איך וועל געדענקען איך וועל געפֿעלן	איך געדענק געדענק! געדענקט! איך געפֿעל געפֿעל! געפֿעלט!	געדענקען געפֿעלן
איך וועל דערציילן איך וועל דערשיסן	איך דערצייל דערצייל! דערציילט! איך דערשיס דערשיס! דערשיסט!	דערציילן דערשיסן
איך וועל פֿאַרקויפֿן איך וועל פֿאַרשטיין איך וועל פֿאַרשפּילן	איך פֿאַרקויף פֿאַרקויף! פֿאַרקויפֿט! איך פֿאַרשטיי פֿאַרשטיי! פֿאַרשטייט! איך פֿאַרשפּיל פֿאַרשפּיל! פֿאַרשפּילט!	פֿאַרקויפֿן פֿאַרשטיין פֿאַרשפּילן
איך וועל צעברעכן	איך צעברעך צעברעך! צעברעכט!	צעברעכן

Past participles of inseparable prefix verbs are never preceded by גע: that place is taken by the unstressed prefix. Verbs that have that prefix as part of their infinitive retain it. Like "weak verbs" that are not prefixed, the default form of the past participle for these verbs is: ט + *verbal base* with the auxiliary האָבן. However, like "strong verbs," there are many instances of base changes and other irregularities.

The same rules for determining the auxiliary apply as for all verbs in the past tense.

Translation	Past tense	Past participle	Verb
I ran away	איך בין אַנטלאָפֿן	אַנטלאָפֿן	אַנטלויפֿן
I decided	איך האָב באַשלאָסן	באַשלאָסן	באַשליסן
I remembered I appealed (to)	איך האָב געדענקט איך בין געפֿעלן	געדענקט געפֿעלן	געדענקען געפֿעלן
I told, recounted I shot (dead)	איך האָב דערציילט איך האָב דערשאָסן	דערציילט דערשאָסן	דערציילן דערשיסן
I understood I sold I misplayed (lost)	איך האָב פֿאַרשטאַנען איך האָב פֿאַרקויפֿט איך האָב פֿאַרשפּילט	פֿאַרשטאַנען פֿאַרקויפֿט פֿאַרשפּילט	פֿאַרשטיין פֿאַרקויפֿן פֿאַרשפּילן
I broke	איך האָב צעבראָכן	צעבראָכן	צעברעכן

Exercise 20.1

Provide the present tense, future tense and past tense conjugations for the complemented verb אויפֿשטיין and the inseparable prefix verb פֿאַרשטיין.

Exercise 20.2

Fill in the blanks in each sentence. The infinitive of the complemented/inseparable prefix verb and tense are indicated in {}. Then provide an English translation.

Reminder: Identify the subject of your verb and make sure that your verb and subject agree in gender and number.

Example:

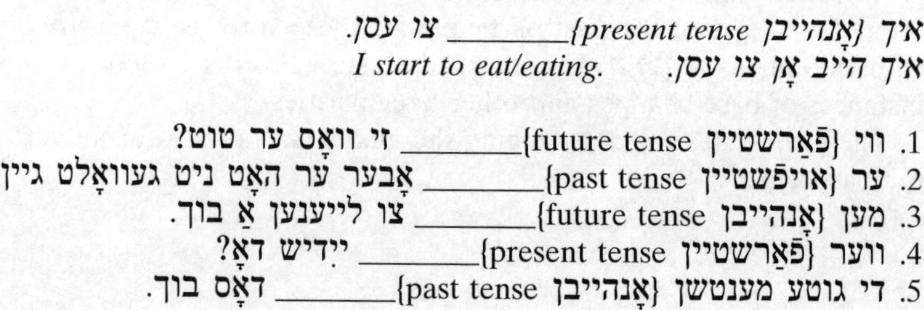

איך *{אָנהייבן present tense}______ צו עסן.*
איך הייב אָן צו עסן. *I start to eat/eating.*

1. ווי {פֿאַרשטיין future tense}______ זי וואָס ער טוט?
2. ער {אויפֿשטיין past tense}______ אָבער ער האָט ניט געוואָלט גיין.
3. מען {אָנהייבן future tense}______ צו לייענען אַ בוך.
4. ווער {פֿאַרשטיין present tense}______ יידיש דאָ?
5. די גוטע מענטשן {אָנהייבן past tense}______ דאָס בוך.

Exercise 20.3

Translate the following sentences into English.

1. איך פֿאַרשטיי פֿאַרוואָס זיי שטייען ניט אויף.
2. מיר ווילן, דו זאָלסט אָנהייבן צו עסן איצט!
3. שטייט אויף און הייבט אָן גיין!
4. מען וועט וויסן אַז ער פֿאַרשטייט גאָרניט.
5. די מענטשן האָבן פֿאַרשטאַנען ווען זיי האָבן געמוזט פֿאָרן.

Exercise 20.4

Translate the following sentences into Yiddish.

1. I am getting up now.
2. Do you (singular, informal) not understand me?
3. People are starting to know about us.
4. Let's get up and go to the park.
5. One wants to begin the book.

UNIT 21

Aspect: repeated action in the past פֿלעגן, aspectual verbal constructions

Repeated action in the past פֿלעגן

The auxiliary verb פֿלעגן is used to indicate that an action took place repeatedly/habitually/on a regular basis in the past ("used to"). פֿלעגן is defective: it carries no meaning on its own and it exists in no other formulation in Yiddish.

infinitive of verb	+	auxiliary verb פֿלעגן	
		איך פֿלעג	מיר פֿלעגן
		דו פֿלעגסט	איר פֿלעגט
		ער/זי/עס/מען פֿלעג	זיי פֿלעגן

Example:

I used to write. איך פֿלעג שרײַבן.

Aspectual verbal constructions

The following constructions convey information about how often/in what way/how long an action takes place. They appear in all tenses and moods.

Singulative aspect

The verbs גיבן, טאָן, כאַפּן, which respectively mean "to give, to do, to grab" in Yiddish, also function as auxiliary verbs in these verbal constructions:

Meaning	Construction			
a quick, one-time act	verbal stem *base of verb/ infinitive minus ending of ן, ען*	אַ	+	*געבן / טאָן
a quick "grabbed/ stolen" act				כאַפּן

*Sometimes but not always interchangeable.

Examples:

I take/have a (quick) read. איך גיב/טו אַ לייען.
I grab a (quick) read. איך כאַפּ אַ לייען.

The inchoative aspect

The verb נעמען, which means "to take" in Yiddish, also functions as an auxiliary verb in this verbal construction:

Meaning	Construction		
beginning of an action	infinitive of verb	+	נעמען (זיך)

Examples:

I start to write. איך נעם שרײַבן.
איך נעם זיך שרײַבן.

Aspectual constructions using the verb האַלטן

The verb האַלטן, which means "to hold" in Yiddish, also functions as an auxiliary verb in these verbal constructions:

Meaning	Construction		
about to *verb*	infinitive of verb	+	האַלטן בײַ
in the middle of *verb*-ing			האַלטן אין
to keep *verb*-ing (iterative aspect)			האַלטן אין איין

Examples:

I am about to eat.	איך האַלט בײַ עסן.
I am in the middle of eating.	איך האַלט אין עסן.
I keep eating (am constantly eating).	איך האַלט אין איין עסן.

Exercise 21.1

Translate the following sentences into English. Note: Take care that your sentences sound like idiomatic English rather than translations of Yiddish.

1. מיר פֿלעגן גיין אין פּאַרק און שפּילן זיך.
2. מען האָט זיך גענומען עסן, האָב איך געמוזט עסן אויך.
3. דער מענטש האָט געכאַפּט אַ שרײַב.
4. זיי האַלטן ניט בײַ לערנען זיך.
5. פֿלעגסטו האַלטן אין איין לייענען?

Exercise 21.2

Translate the following sentences into Yiddish.

1. My mother used to read us nice books.
2. Let's have a quick read (literally: Let's grab a read!).
3. They want us to be constantly writing.
4. I shall not be in the middle of eating.
5. We used not to sleep.

UNIT 22

The conditional mood

Verbs in the conditional mood express an action that is hypothetical and contingent on a given set of circumstances: *if* + subjunctive mood.

Formulations of the conditional mood

The conjunction *if* אויב is often used before a conditional clause such as "if I go, if I were to go, if I had gone." The conjunctions ווען or אַז can also be used to mean "if."

There are different formulations of the conditional mood in Yiddish that fall into the following basic categories (there are other, lesser-used forms that are not discussed here).

1. Future conditional: a hypothetical statement with the outcome situated in the future tense. The conjunction *if* אויב is used to indicate the conditional nature of the sentence.

Examples:

If I eat, I am going home.	אויב איך עס, גיי איך אַהיים.
When I eat, I go home.	ווען איך עס, גיי איך אַהיים.
If I eat, I shall go home.	אויב איך עס, וועל איך גיין אַהיים.
	ווען איך עס, וועל איך גיין אַהיים.

2. Present conditional: a hypothetical statement with the outcome situated in the present tense. It is expressed using the auxiliary verb וואָלטן.

The present conditional וואָלטן

past participle of verb Less commonly, the infinitive of the verb is used instead of the past participle	+	auxiliary verb וואָלטן איך וואָלט / מיר וואָלטן דו וואָלטסט / איר וואָלט ער/זי/עס/מען וואָלט / זיי וואָלטן

Example:

I would eat/[if] I were to eat — איך וואָלט געגעסן

Another present conditional formulation uses the conjunction *when*, *if* ווען. This formulation can also refer to situations in the past.

Example:

If I were happy — ווען איך בין פֿריילעך

This formulation can also refer to situations in the past.

3. Past conditional: a hypothetical statement with the outcome situated in the past tense. The past conditional can be formed in the same way as the present conditional.

Example:

I would have eaten. — איך וואָלט געגעסן.

Formulations using the pluperfect tense do exist in Yiddish but they are less commonly used:

I would have written. — איך וואָלט געהאַט געשריבן.

Reminder: Subordinate clauses that precede a main clause are treated as single sentence units. The inflected verb in the main clause must appear first so that it remains the second sentence unit.

Example:

If I wanted to, I would eat.
If I had wanted to, I would have eaten. — אויב איך וואָלט געוואָלט, **וואָלט** איך געגעסן.

Note the difference in word order when the conjunction appears between the two clauses:

I would eat if I wanted to.
I would have eaten if I had wanted to. — איך וואָלט געגעסן **אויב** איך וואָלט געוואָלט.

Exercise 22.1

Render the following phrases into the conditional using the past conditional form with the auxiliary verb וואָלטן. Then translate the conditional form into English.

Example:

איך שלאָף
איך וואָלט געשלאָפֿן I would sleep/I would have slept.

1. די מאַמעס פֿאָרן
2. מען האָט ליב
3. דו ביסט
4. דער מענטש ווערט
5. איר לערנט

Exercise 22.2

Create "if-then" sentences in the future, present, and past conditional forms based on the pairs of clauses below using the conjunction אויב and consecutive word order (conjugated verb first in the second clause). Retain the tense of the original clauses: if they are in the future, use the future conditional, if they are in the present, use the present conditional, if they are in the past, use the past conditional. Then translate each of your conditional sentences into English.

Reminder: Be sure to adhere to the rules of word order regarding pronouns in the accusative and dative cases and the negative particle ניט; they go between the inflected and uninflected parts of the verb.

Examples:

איך וועל לייענען, איך וועל שלאָפֿן
אויב איך לייען, שלאָף איך. — *If I read, I shall sleep.*

איך לייען, איך שלאָף
אויב איך וואָלט געלייענט, וואָלט איך געשלאָפֿן. — *If I were to read, I would sleep.*

איך האָב געלייענט, איך האָב געשלאָפֿן
אויב איך וואָלט געלייענט, וואָלט איך געשלאָפֿן. — *If I had read, I would have slept.*

1. מען שפּילט זיך, מען לייענט ניט
2. זיי זײַנען געפֿאָרן, זיי האָבן געגעסן
3. דו וועסט ווערן פֿריילעך, דו וועסט זײַן אַ גוטער מענטש
4. איר האָט געוווּסט וועגן אונדז, איר האָט אונדז ניט ליב געהאַט
5. די מאַמע שטייט אויף, זי הייבט אָן צו לערנען זיך

Exercise 22.3

Translate the following sentences into English. Some sentences may have more than one translation.

1. ווען איך וואָלט פֿאַרשטאַנען דאָס בוך, וואָלט איך עס טאַקע ליב געהאַט.
2. אויב מען הייבט אָן צו עסן שיין, וועט עס זייַן גוט.
3. מיר וואָלטן זיך ניט געשפּילט אין פּאַרק מיט זיי!
4. איר וואָלט אויפֿגעשטאַנען אויב איר וואָלט געמוזט.
5. וואָלטסטו געגאַנגען מיט דעם מענטשן?

Exercise 22.4

Translate the following sentences into Yiddish.

1. I would not go.
2. If I could, I would do it.
3. One would not have been permitted to have any books./No books would have been permitted.
4. If I am reading, I will be happy.
5. Whom would we play with?

UNIT 23

The participle and suffixes on nouns, adjectives and verbs

A participle

The participle is a word formed from a verb that has no tense. Uninflected it can function as an adverb. It can also inflect as an adjective.

Examples:

1. The children are in bed **sleeping**.

   Sleeping is an adverb: it answers the questions where, how, in what manner?

2. The **sleeping** children are in bed.

   Sleeping is an adjective: it describes the children.

There are two forms of Yiddish participles: the present participle and the past participle.

1. The present participle

The present participle can function as an adverb or adjective (gerund).

Formation of the present participle

ending of נדיק ענדיק after a stressed vowel or the following consonants: ל, נ, מ, נג, נק	+	base of verb *infinitive minus ending of ן, ען*

As an adverb, the participle does not inflect.

Examples:

I am reading a book **(while) eating**.	**עסנדיק** לייען איך אַ בוך. איך לייען אַ בוך **עסנדיק**.
They are reading a book **(while) eating**.	**עסנדיק** לייענען זיי אַ בוך. זיי לייענען אַ בוך **עסנדיק**.

As an adjective (gerund) the participle inflects like a regular adjective: it declines according to gender, number and case.

Examples:

The eating person (the person who is eating) is reading a book.	*masculine, singular, nominative*	**דער עסנדיקער** מענטש לייענט אַ בוך.
The eating mother (the mother who is eating) is reading a book.	*feminine, singular, nominative*	**די עסנדיקע** מאַמע לייענט אַ בוך.
I know **the eating** person (the person who is eating).	*masculine, singular, accusative*	איך קען **דעם עסנדיקן** מענטשן.
One knows about **the eating mother** (the mother who is eating).	*feminine, singular, dative*	מען ווייס וועגן **דער עסנדיקער** מאַמע.

Note: Many, but not all verbs can use this adjectival form.

2. The past participle

The past participle functions as an adjective to indicate a passive state.

Formation of the past participle

ending on adjective base *declined according to gender, number and case*	+	past participle

Examples using the regular verb דרוקן *to print* (past participle: געדרוקט)*:

The printed book is big/large.	**דאָס געדרוקטע** בוך איז גרויס.
I have **the printed** book.	איך האָב **דאָס געדרוקטע** בוך.
I know about **the printed** book.	איך ווייס וועגן **דעם געדרוקטן** בוך.

*This verb does not form part of this text's working vocabulary except in the exercises for this chapter.

In all of these cases, "the printed book" refers to "the book that has been printed." That is, the book is described by its quality of having been printed.

Note: In this usage, the past participle of the verb *to be* זײַן is געווען. It means "former, past."

Suffixes on nouns, adjectives and verbs

Yiddish has many ways of forming new words by adding suffixes onto nouns, adjectives and verbs.

Many of the suffixes are productive: they can be used to create new words.

Examples of Yiddish suffixes

Suffixes that form nouns impart gender. Genders are indicated next to the relevant examples.

Note: Only the noun שרײַבער forms part of this text's working vocabulary.

Translation	Example	Function	Attached to a	Suffix
humanity	די מענטשהייט	abstract noun	noun	־הייט
reading material	דאָס לייענוואַרג	material related to the noun, verbal base, adjective	noun, verbal base, adjective	־וואַרג
female writer	די שרײַבערין	renders a noun feminine	noun	־ין
belonging to the category/ characteristic of writers (on שרײַבער see below)	שרײַבעריש	adjectives that indicate belonging to a category	noun	־יש
scribbling	דאָס שרײַבעכץ	derogatory	verbal stem	־עכץ
little, beloved Motl (can also be used pejoratively) secular book	מאָטעלע מאָטקעניו מאָטקעלע מאָטקעשי ... דאָס ביכל	diminutive	noun often used with proper name; often cause of vowel changes; sometimes used in combination	־(ע)לע ־ניו ־קע ־ש ...

Translation	Example	Function	Attached to	Suffix
writer (a person who writes)	דער שרײַבער	a noun referring to the performer of an action	a verbal stem	־ער
New Yorker (person; quality)	דער ניו־יאָרקער	invariant adjective: of/from that place	names of cities, town, countries	־ער
greatness	די גרויסקייט	noun that is characterized by the adjective	an adjective	־קייט

Exercise 23.1

In each sentence make the infinitive provided in {} into a participle. The {} also indicates whether it should be a present participle or a past participle.

If the present participle is an adverb, leave it in its base form. If it is an adjective, be sure to add the correct adjectival endings as needed. Past participles will agree with their nouns in gender, number and case.

Example:

די {עסן *present participle*}_______ מאַמעס לערנען זיך.
די עסנדיקע מאַמעס לערנען זיך. *The eating mothers are studying.*

1. {שלאָפֿן present participle}_______איז ער געגאַנגען אין פּאַרק.
2. ווו איז דאָס {דרוקן past participle}_______בוך?
3. ווער איז דער {שרײַבן present participle}_______מענטשעלע?
4. גיב מיר דאָס {שרײַבן past participle}_______ביכל!
5. די מענטשן גייען {עסן present participle}_______.

Exercise 23.2

Translate the sentences in 23.1 into English. Note: Q.4 has a noun with a diminutive ending.

Exercise 23.3

Translate the following sentences into Yiddish. Participles are indicated in **bold**.

1. **Knowing** that it was not good, I read the book.
2. The **read** book is not here.
3. One may not/is not permitted to write while **walking**!
4. The **understanding** people are starting to go.
5. We know that, **having** one book, he is happy.

UNIT 24
Demonstrative pronouns

Demonstrative pronouns

Demonstrative pronouns substitute nouns that are clearly indicated by the context.

In Yiddish they include: this; that; an/the other.

"This/these"

As discussed in Unit 1, implicit "this/these" is identical to the definite article with added stress. "This-ness" can be underlined via word order with the "this" phrase as the first sentence unit. In writing, this-ness can be clearly indicated by using a different font: italicized or spaced apart letters (commonly used in printed Yiddish sources as italics) or bold font.

Examples:

You like the writer.	איר האָט ליב דעם שרײַבער.
You like this writer.	דעם שרײַבער האָט איר ליב.
You like *this* writer.	איר האָט ליב *דעם שרײַבער*.
You like **this** writer.	איר האָט ליב **דעם שרײַבער**.

Explicit "this/these" is indicated using the following formulations:

1. The inflected adjectival form דאָזיק.
2. Placing the particle אָט before the definite article. אָט placed after the inflected form of דאָזיק adds emphasis. אָט אָ in this position offers even greater emphasis.

Examples:

דער דאָזיקער מענטש
אָט דער מענטש
אָט אָ דער מענטש

אָט דער דאָזיקער מענטש
אָט אָ דער דאָזיקער מענטש

"That/those"

Stressed definite articles can also carry a connotation of "that/those."

Explicit "that/those" can be indicated using the inflected adjectival form יענער, which means "that".

יענער declines as follows:

Declension of יענער

Dative	Accusative	Nominative	
יענעם	יענעם	יענער	Masculine
יענער	יענע	יענע	Feminine
יענעם	יענץ	יענץ	Neuter
יענע	יענע	יענע	Plural

Examples:

That person is nice/attractive. יענער מענטש איז שיין.
I love that writer. איך האָב ליב יענעם שרײַבער.
Those books are written about. מען שרײַבט וועגן יענע ביכער.

The possessive form of יענער is יענעמס.

Example:

I have that [person's] books. איך האָב יענעמס ביכער.

"Other"

The concept of "other, אַנדער" in Yiddish has two different constructions: "another" and "the other."

1. "Another"

When using the adjective "other" to refer to a noun that is not preceded by the definite article "the", אַנדער only inflects in the singular and plural (like possessive adjectives).

It does not decline according to gender and case.

"Another"

אַנדער	+	אַן	singular
אַנדערע		-	plural

Examples:

I am reading another book. איך לייען **אַן** אַנדער בוך.
I am reading some other books. איך לייען **אַנדערע** ביכער.

"The other"

The Yiddish attributive adjective "other" can indicate "that-ness" for a noun. It can also stand in for a noun (that one, those ones).

When using the adjective "other" to refer to a noun that is preceded by the definite article "the", **אַנדער** inflects according to gender and case like any other adjective.

Example:

The other man is eating.	*masculine, singular, nominative*	**דער אַנדערער** מענטש עסט.
I know the other park.	*masculine, singular, accusative*	איך קען **דעם אַנדערן** פּאַרק.
I am the other (woman).	*feminine, singular nominative*	איך בין **די אַנדערע**.
I am traveling to the other city.	*feminine, singular, dative*	איך פֿאָר אין **דער אַנדערער** שטאָט.
I am reading the other book.	*neuter, singular, accusative*	איך לייען **דאָס אַנדערע** בוך.
I am reading the other books.	*neuter, plural, accusative*	איך לייען **די אַנדערע** ביכער.

Exercise 24.1

In each sentence, identify the verb, subject, direct object, indirect object and prepositions. If the noun phrase containing the _______ is definite (starts with the word "the"), provide the gender, number and case.

Then provide the correct forms of the attributive adjective **אַנדער**.

Example:

איך בין די _______*מאַמע.*

Verb: בין
Subject 1: איך
Subject 2: מאַמע (predicate noun): feminine, singular, nominative

איך בין די *אַנדערע* מאַמע.

1. אַן _______מענטש איז געפֿאָרן.
2. מען גיט אונדז דעם _______ שרײַבער.
3. ווער איז אין דער _______שטאָט?
4. זיי שרײַבן וועגן די _______ מענטשן.
5. מיר ווילן _______ ביכער!

Exercise 24.2

Provide the correct forms of the attributive adjective **יענער**.

Then translate each sentence into English.

Example:

איך בין _______ *מאַמע.*
איך בין *יענע* מאַמע.

I am that mother.

1. _______מענטש איז געפֿאָרן.
2. מען גיט אונדז _______ ביכער.
3. ווער איז אין _______שטאָט?
4. זיי שרײַבן וועגן _______ מענטשן.
5. מיר ווילן _______ ביכער!

Exercise 24.3

Translate the following sentences into Yiddish.

1. The mother is reading the other book.
2. One does not want to travel to that particular city.
3. One wants another one! (Another one is wanted!)
4. That one [person] is the great writer.
5. Where is the other one's [person's] book?

UNIT 25

Comparative and superlative adjectives

Comparative and superlative adjectives express comparison, either between two nouns (example: she is better than him) or between a noun and all other nouns (example: she is the best).

Comparative adjectives

Comparative adjectives are used to compare two nouns.
Example: he is bigger than me.

Forming comparative adjectives

Case of noun to which it is being compared		Preposition		Adjective being compared
dative	+	פֿון or פֿאַר	+	ער + base form of adjective
nominative		ווי		

Which of the above forms to use is a matter of personal style. For example, some Yiddish stylists prefer not to use the form with the preposition פֿון because that preposition already appears very frequently in the language.

Examples of the forms:

The person is **happier than you.** .דער מענטש איז פֿריילעכער פֿאַר דיר
.דער מענטש איז פֿריילעכער פֿון דיר
.דער מענטש איז פֿריילעכער ווי דו

Adjective bases often change stems in the comparative, in particular adjectives whose base forms one syllable. The list is extensive.

Vocabulary: examples of comparatives with base changes

Translation	Comparative form	Adjective
better	בעסער	גוט
greater, larger	גרעסער	גרויס
smaller	קלענער	קליין
nicer, more attractive	שענער	שיין

Examples:

The person is **better than you**. דער מענטש איז **בעסער פֿאַר דיר**.
דער מענטש איז **בעסער פֿון דיר**.
דער מענטש איז **בעסער ווי דו**.

Adjectives with more than three syllables are formed as follows:

Case of noun to which it is being compared	+	Preposition	+	Adjective being compared	+	מער
dative		פֿאַר/ פֿון		base form of adjective		
nominative		ווי				

Example: the adjective *interesting* *אינטערעסאַנט*

The person is **more interesting than you**. דער מענטש איז **מער אינטערעסאַנט פֿאַר דיר**.
דער מענטש איז **מער אינטערעסאַנט פֿון דיר**.
דער מענטש איז **מער אינטערעסאַנט ווי דו**.

As predicate adjectives, comparative adjectives are formed as follows:

ending on adjective base *declined according to gender, number and case*	+	ער	+	base form of adjective	+	definite article of noun

Example:

The person is the better (one). דער מענטש איז **דער בעסערער**.

Comparative adjectives can also be used as adverbs. Like other adjectives, they appear in their base forms and do not inflect.

Example:

He should eat/be eating **better**. ער זאָל עסן **בעסער**.

Superlative adjectives

Superlative adjectives are used to express the highest degree of an adjective.

Examples:

He is the biggest.
He has the biggest house.

Forming superlative adjectives

Ending on adjective base *declined according to gender, number and case*	+	סט	+	Base form of adjective	+	Definite article of noun

The article and superlative adjective ending will agree with the noun in gender, number, and case.

Superlative adjectives can appear as predicate or attributive adjectives.

Examples:

The person is **the happiest**. דער מענטש איז **דער פֿריילעכסטער**.
I know **the happiest** park. איך קען **דעם פֿריילעכסטן** פּאַרק.
The mother is **the happiest**. די מאַמע איז **די פֿריילעכסטע**.
I am traveling to **the happiest** city. איך פֿאָר אין **דער פֿריילעכסטער** שטאָט.
The book is **the happiest**. דאָס בוך איז **דאָס פֿריילעכסטע**.
I am reading **the happiest** books. איך לייען **די פֿריילעכסטע** ביכער.

Note: Adjectives that have base changes in the comparative will also have them in the superlative.

Examples:

The person is **the best**. דער מענטש איז **דער בעסטער**.
I know **the best** park. איך קען **דעם בעסטן** פּאַרק.

Exercise 25.1

Rewrite the adjective in each sentence in the comparative. Adjectives appear in bold.

Example:

Comparative	Base form
ער איז פֿריילעכער.	ער איז פֿריילעך.

1. דו האָסט אַ **שיינע** מאַמע.
2. מען שרײַבט וועגן **גוטע** ביכער.
3. ער לייענט אַ **גרויסן** שרײַבער.
4. ווער איז **גוט**?
5. די **קליינע** ביכער זײַנען דאָ.

Exercise 25.2

Rewrite the adjective in each sentence in 25.1 in the superlative.

Example:

Superlative	Base form
ער איז דער פֿריילעכסטער.	ער איז פֿריילעך.

Exercise 25.3

Translate the following sentences into English.

1. דער מענטש איז אַ ביסל הונגעריקער פֿאַר מיר.
2. דאָס בעסטע בוך שרײַב איך!
3. איז ער שענער ווי זי?
4. מען פֿאָרט אין אַ בעסערער שטאָט.
5. ער איז דער גרעסטער שרײַבער.

GLOSSARY OF WORKING VOCABULARY

Terms employed in examples and exercises

All vocabulary is listed in Yiddish alphabetical order with its part of speech indicated and with English translation(s). Nouns are listed with their genders (m, f, n) and plural forms. Adjectives are listed in their base forms. Verbs are listed in their infinitive forms, with irregular present tense or past tense conjugations indicated.

Translation	Part of speech	Yiddish
a little	adjective quantifier	אַ ביסל
but	conjunction	אָבער
or	conjunction	אָדער
there (thither)	adverb	אַהין
here (hither)	adverb	אַהער
if, whether	conjunction	אויב
and	conjunction	און
on (also: at, for, etc.)	preposition	אויף
to get up/stand up	verb (complemented)	אויפֿשטיין
that, when	conjunction	אַז
so (not "therefore")	adverb	אַזוי
to begin	verb (complemented)	אָנהייבן
in	preposition	אין
now	adverb	איצט
all	adverb	אַלע

Translation	Part of speech	Yiddish
book	noun	בוך (n) ביכער
until	conjunction	ביז
at (someone's)	preposition	בײַ
nothing	pronoun	גאָרניט
good	adjective	גוט
to go/travel on foot	verb	גיין – איז געגאַנגען
to give	verb	געבן – גיב – געגעבן
to like, to appeal to	verb (inseparable prefix)	געפֿעלן
big, great	adjective	גרויס
here	adverb	דאָ
here (hence)	adverb	דאַנען
there/there (thither)	adverb	דאָרט/דאָרטן
to need, have to	verb (modal verb)	דאַרפֿן
therefore, then	adverb	דערפֿאַר
to have	verb	האָבן – געהאַט
home	noun	היים (f) היימען
where (whence)	adverb	וואַנען
what	interrogative pronoun	וואָס
which	interrogative pronoun	וואָסער
where	question word/adverb	ווּ
where (whither)	adverb	ווּהין
how	question word	ווי
how, in what way	question word	ווי אַזוי
because	conjunction	ווײַל
to know	verb	וויסן – ווייס – געוווּסט
how much/many	question word	וויפֿל
about	preposition	וועגן
to want	verb (modal verb)	וועלן – געוואָלט

Translation	Part of speech	Yiddish
when	question word	ווען
to become	verb	ווערן – איז געוואָרן
ought, should	verb (modal verb)	זאָלן
to be	verb	זײַן – איך בין... – איז געווען
very	adjective quantifier	זייער
wedding (*khasene -khasenes*)	noun	חתונה (f) חתונות
therefore, so *questions, commands	conjunction	טאָ
really, truly	adverb	טאַקע
to do	verb	טאָן – טו – געטאָן
to be forbidden from	verb (modal verb)	טאָרן ניט
Yiddish/Jewish	noun/adjective	ייִדיש
each, every	pronoun	יעדער
although	conjunction	כאָטש
to read	verb	לייענען
to teach	verb	לערנען
to study	verb	לערנען זיך
Yiddish name: Motl	noun	מאָטל
mother	noun	מאַמע (f) מאַמעס
must	verb (modal verb)	מוזן
with	preposition	מיט
to be allowed to, may	verb (modal verb)	מעגן
person	noun	מענטש (m) מענטשן
New York	noun	ניו־יאָרק
to be forbidden from	verb (modal verb)	ניט טאָרן
either...or	conjunction	סײַ...סײַ
someone	pronoun	עמעצער
to eat	verb	עסן – געגעסן

Translation	Part of speech	Yiddish
for/before/in front of	preposition	פֿאַר
why	question word	פֿאַרוואָס
to go/travel by vehicle	verb	פֿאָרן – איז געפֿאָרן
to understand	verb (inseparable prefix)	פֿאַרשטיין
from	preposition	פֿון
happy	adjective	פֿריילעך
to	preposition	צו
not (any)	particle	קיין
no one	pronoun	קיינער
to (a place)	preposition	קיין
class	noun	קלאַס (m) קלאַסן
small	adjective	קליין
to know how to, be able to	verb (modal verb)	קענען
already	adverb	שוין
nice, attractive	adjective	שיין
city	noun	שטאָט (f) שטעט
to sleep	verb	שלאָפֿן – געשלאָפֿן
to play (with something/one)	verb	שפּילן
to play	verb	שפּילן זיך
to write	verb	שרײַבן – געשריבן
writer	noun	שרײַבער (m) שרײַבערס

KEY TO EXERCISES

Unit 1

Exercise 1.1

1. בוך gender: neuter; number: singular; case: nominative
2. מענטשן gender: masculine; number: plural; case: nominative
3. מאַמעס gender: feminine; number: plural; case: nominative
4. ביכער gender: neuter; number: plural; case: nominative
5. מענטש gender: masculine; number: singular; case: nominative

Exercise 1.2

1. בוך neuter, singular, nominative
   דאָס גוטע בוך \ אַ גוט בוך
2. ביכער neuter, plural, nominative
   די גוטע ביכער \ גוטע ביכער
3. מאַמע feminine, singular, nominative
   די גוטע מאַמע \ אַ גוטע מאַמע
4. מאַמעס feminine, plural, nominative
   די גוטע מאַמעס \ גוטע מאַמעס
5. מענטשן masculine, plural, nominative
   די גוטע מענטשן \ גוטע מענטשן

Exercise 1.3

1. די מאַמעס feminine, plural, nominative
   זי The pronoun is third person, feminine, plural, nominative
2. דאָס גרויסע בוך neuter, singular, nominative
   עס The pronoun is third person, neuter, singular, nominative
3. שיינע מענטשן masculine, plural, nominative
   זיי The pronoun is third person, masculine, plural, nominative
4. די ביכער neuter, plural, nominative
   זיי The pronoun is third person, neuter, plural, nominative
5. אַ פֿריילעכע מאַמע feminine, singular, nominative
   זי The pronoun is third person, feminine, singular, nominative

Exercise 1.4

1. the small books
2. a/any happy person
3. good mothers
4. the nice books
5. the great mother

Exercise 1.5

1. דאָס גרויסע בוך
2. אַ קליין בוך
3. די גוטע מאַמע
4. אַ שיינער מענטש
5. פֿריילעכע מענטשן

Unit 2

Exercise 2.1

1. ווערן
איך ווער, דו ווערסט, ער/זי/עס/מען ווערט, מיר ווערן, איר ווערט, זיי ווערן.
2. עסן
איך עס, דו עסט, ער/זי/עס/מען עסט, מיר עסן, איר עסט, זיי עסן.
3. לייענען
איך לייען, דו לייענסט, ער/זי/עס/מען לייענט, מיר לייענען, איר לייענט, זיי לייענען.
4. שלאָפֿן
איך שלאָף, דו שלאָפֿסט, ער/זי/עס/מען שלאָפֿט, מיר שלאָפֿן, איר שלאָפֿט, זיי שלאָפֿן.

Exercise 2.2

1. איך ווער first person singular
2. זי שלאָפֿט third person singular
3. מיר עסן first person plural
4. איר לייענט second person plural
5. זיי ווערן third person plural
6. מען שרײַבט third person singular
7. דו ווערסט second person singular
8. ער לייענט third person singular

Exercise 2.3

1. מיר עסן. person: first person; number: plural
2. די מענטשן שרײַבן. person: third person; number: plural

3. עס ווערט גרויס. person: third person; number: singular
4. מען לייענט. person: third person; number: singular
5. איך שלאָף. person: first person; number: singular

Exercise 2.4

1. We eat/are eating.
2. The people write/are writing.
3. It becomes/is becoming great/large.
4. One reads/is reading.
5. I sleep/am sleeping.

Exercise 2.5

1. דער גרויסער מענטש לייענט.
2. זיי ווערן פֿריילעך.
3. די קליינע מאַמע עסט.
4. מיר לייענען.
5. מען לייענט אַ שיין בוך.

Unit 3

Exercise 3.1

1. מיר זײַנען גרויס.
2. די מאַמע איז גרויס. *זי
3. איך בין גרויס.
4. אַלע ביכער זײַנען גרויס. *זיי
5. דו ביסט גרויס.
6. איר זײַט גרויס.
7. עס איז גרויס.
8. מען איז גרויס.
9. ער איז גרויס.
10. זיי זײַנען גרויס.

Exercise 3.2

1. איך ווער אַ פֿריילעכער מענטש.
- verb: ווער present indicative tense, first person, singular
- subject noun/pronoun: איך first person, singular.
- predicate noun: אַ פֿריילעכער מענטש

2. זיי זײַנען גוטע ביכער.
- verb: זײַנען present indicative tense, third person, plural

*Note: Although the forms are identical, זײַנען is third person plural and not first person plural because it "agrees" with זיי as well as ביכער , both of which are third person plural.

– subject noun/pronoun: זײ plural.
– predicate noun: גוטע ביכער masculine, plural.

3. דער מענטש איז אַ שײנער.

– verb: איז present indicative tense, third person, singular.
– subject noun/pronoun: דער מענטש masculine, singular.
– predicate adjective: אַ שײנער masculine, singular.

4. גוטע מענטשן זײַנען פֿרײלעך.

– verb: זײַנען present indicative tense, third person, plural (can also be first person plural; see *note above)
– subject noun/pronoun: גוטע מענטשן masculine, plural, nominative.
– predicate adjective: פֿרײלעך

5. דאָס בוך װערט גוט.

– verb: װערט present indicative tense, third person, singular (can also be second person plural; see *note above)
– subject noun/pronoun: דאָס בוך neuter, singular.
– predicate adjective: גוט

Exercise 3.3

1. I am becoming a happy person.
2. These are good books.
3. The person is a very nice/attractive one.
4. Good people are happy.
5. The book is becoming good.

Exercise 3.4

1. איך בין גרױס!
2. דער קלײנער איז פֿרײלעך.
3. זי איז אַ גוטער מענטש.
4. דאָס בוך איז אַ קלײנס.
5. די מאַמע איז קלײן.

Unit 4

Exercise 4.1

1. Adverbs: אַלע, שױן
   Translation: The people all read already./The people are all reading already.
2. Adverbs: אַזױ, שײן
   Translation: You eat/are eating so nicely.

3. Adverb: גוט
   Translation: We sleep/are sleeping well.
4. Adverbs: איצט, דאָ
   Translation: I am already here now.
5. Adverb: זייער
   Translation: The mother is becoming a very happy one (woman).

Exercise 4.2

1. זיי לייענען טאַקע גוט.
2. איך עס פֿריילעך.
3. זי שרײַבט איצט.
4. איר זײַט אַ ביסל קליין.
5. מיר זײַנען אַלע זייער פֿריילעכע מענטשן.

Unit 5

Exercise 5.1

1. 14
2. 27
3. 151
4. 3
5. 69

Exercise 5.2

1. דרײַ הונדערט דרײַ און דרײַסיק
2. זיבעצן
3. איינס
4. טויזנט נײַן הונדערט אַכט און זיבעציק
5. מיליאָן, פֿינף הונדערט אַכט און זעכציק טויזנט, צוויי הונדערט און צוועלף

Exercise 5.3

1. זעקס ביכער
2. איין מאַמע
3. דער צווייטער מענטש
4. נײַן און נײַנציק מענטשן
5. דאָס אַכט און פֿופֿציקסטע בוך

Unit 6

Exercise 6.1

1. איר בוך
2. זייערע מאַמעס
3. אונדזער מענטש
4. דײַנע ביכער
5. אײַערע מענטשן

Exercise 6.2

1. ביכער = *neuter, plural*
   זײַנע שיינע ביכער
   His nice books
2. מענטש = *masculine, singular*
   אונדזער גרויסער מענטש
   Our great person
3. מאַמע = *feminine, singular*
   זייער שיינע מאַמע
   Their nice/attractive mother
4. מאַמעס = *feminine, plural*
   דײַנע גוטע מאַמעס
   Your (singular) good mothers
5. בוך = *neuter, singular*
   איר קליין בוך
   Her small book

Exercise 6.3

1. Possessive adjective: first person singular = מײַן
   Attributive adjective (agreeing with בוך): neuter, singular, nominative = גרויס
   Noun: neuter, singular, nominative = בוך
   Verb in the present indicative: third person, singular to agree with בוך = איז
   Adverb: זייער
   Predicate adjective = גוט
   Sentence in the plural: אונדזערע גרויסע ביכער זײַנען גוט.

2. Possessive adjective: singular = זײַן
   Noun: feminine, singular, nominative = מאַמע
   Verb in the present indicative: third person, singular to agree with מאַמע = לייענט
   Adverb: שיין
   Sentence in the plural: .זייערע מאַמעס לייענען שיין

3. Definite article: neuter, singular, nominative = דאָס
   Attributive adjective (agreeing with בוך): neuter, singular, nominative = שיינע
   Noun: neuter, singular, nominative = בוך
   Verb in the present indicative: third person, singular to agree with בוך = ווערט
   Possessive pronouns in the predicate (neuter, singular) = מײַנס
   Sentence in the plural: .די שיינע ביכער ווערן אונדזערע

4. Personal pronoun: first person singular = איך
   Verb in the present indicative: first person, singular to agree with איך = ווער
   Predicate nominative (masculine, singular, nominative) = אַ גוטער מענטש
   Sentence in the plural: .מיר ווערן גוטע מענטשן

5. Personal pronoun: second person singular = דו
   Verb in the present indicative: second person, singular to agree with דו = ביסט
   Possessive adjective: third person feminine, singular = איר
   Predicate nominative (feminine, singular, nominative) = מאַמע
   Sentence in the plural: .איר זײַט זייערע מאַמעס

Exercise 6.4

	Singular	Plural
1.	My big book is good.	Our big books are good.
2.	His mother is reading nicely.	Their mothers are reading nicely.
3.	The nice book is becoming mine.	The nice books are becoming ours.
4.	I am becoming a happy person.	We are becoming happy people.
5.	You are her mother.	You (plural) are their mothers.

Exercise 6.5

1. זייער מאַמע עסט פֿריילעך.
2. מײַן בוך איז אַזוי גוט!
3. אונדזער מאַמע שלאָפֿט גוט.
4. זײַנע מענטשן שרײַבן אַ ביסל.
5. מײַנער אַ קלאַס איז טאַקע גוט.

Unit 7

Exercise 7.1

1. דער מענטש עסט ניט.
2. זי לייענט ניט איצט.
3. זיי ווערן ניט גרויס.
4. איך שלאָף ניט גוט.
5. מיר שרײַבן ניט שיין.

Exercise 7.2

Original	Negated
1. The person eats/is eating.	The person does not eat/is not eating.
2. She reads/is reading now.	She does not read/is not reading now.
3. They become/are becoming great.	They do not become/are not becoming great.
4. I sleep/am sleeping well.	I do not sleep/am not sleeping well.
5. We write/are writing nicely.	We do not write/are not writing nicely.

Exercise 7.3

1. ער ווערט ניט דער גוטער מענטש.
2. ער ווערט ניט קיין גוטער מענטש.
3. זיי ווערן ניט די גוטע מענטשן.
4. זיי ווערן ניט קיין גוטע מענטשן.
5. אונדזער מאַמע איז ניט די שיינע.
6. אונדזער מאַמע איז ניט קיין שיינע.
7. אונדזערע מאַמעס זײַנען ניט די שיינע.
8. אונדזערע מאַמעס זײַנען ניט קיין שיינע.

Exercise 7.4

Original	Negated
1. He becomes/is becoming the good person.	He does not become/is not becoming the good person.

2. He becomes/is becoming a good person.	He does not become/is not becoming a (any) good person.
3. They become/are becoming the good people.	They do not become/are not becoming the good people.
4. They become/are becoming good people.	They do not become/are not becoming (any) good people.
5. Our mother is the nice/attractive one (woman).	Our mother is not the nice/ attractive one (woman).
6. Our mother is a nice/attractive one (woman).	Our mother is not a (any) nice/ attractive one (woman).
7. Ours mother are the nice/ attractive ones (women).	Our mothers are not the nice/ attractive ones (women).
8. Our mothers are nice/attractive ones (women).	Our mothers are not a (any) nice/ attractive ones (women).

Exercise 7.5

1. ער איז ניט קיין פֿרײלעכער מענטש.
2. דאָס בוך איז ניט אַזוי גוט.
3. זײער מאַמע איז ניט זײער שײן.
4. אונדזער בוך איז ניט טאַקע קלײן.
5. מיר זײַנען ניט די קלײנע מענטשן.

Unit 8

Exercise 8.1

1. איך בין ניט דאָ / ניטאָ.
2. מיר שלאָפֿן אַלע איצט.
3. די פֿרײלעכע מענטשן עסן אַ ביסל.
4. זי װערט טאַקע אַ גוטע מאַמע.
5. מען לײענט די גרױסע ביכער.
6. אונדזערע ביכער זײַנען ניט קײן גוטע.
7. ער איז אַזוי שײן.
8. איצט שרײַבט איר.

Exercise 8.2

1. I am not here.
2. We are all sleeping now.
3. The happy people eat/are eating a little.
4. She is becoming a really/truly good mother.
5. One reads the great/large books./The great/large books are being read.

6. Our books are not good ones.
7. He is so nice/attractive.
8. Now you (plural/formal) write/are writing.

Exercise 8.3

1. בין איך ניט דאָ / ניטאָ?
2. שלאָפֿן מיר אַלע איצט?
3. עסן די פֿריילעכע מענטשן אַ ביסל?
4. ווערט זי טאַקע אַ גוטע מאַמע?
5. לייענט מען די גרויסע ביכער?
6. זייַנען אונדזערע ביכער ניט קיין גוטע?
7. איז ער אַזוי שיין?
8. שרייַבט איר איצט?

Exercise 8.4

1. Am I not here?
2. Are we all sleeping now?
3. Are the happy people eating a little/Do the happy people eat a little?
4. Is she becoming a really/truly good mother?
5. Does one read/Is one reading the great/large books?/Are the great/large books being read?
6. Are our books not good ones?
7. Is he so nice/attractive?
8. Do you (plural/formal) write/Are you (plural/formal) writing now?

Exercise 8.5

1. ווען עסטו? / ווען עסט איר?
2. פֿאַרוואָס איז זי דאָ?
3. ווער זייַנען די מענטשן?
4. ווי לייענט מען ניט דאָס גרויסע בוך?
5. וואָס עסט עס?
6. וויפֿל שלאָפֿן די מאַמעס?
7. וווּ בין איך?
8. שרייַבסטו?
9. זייַנען די ביכער אונדזערע?
10. בין איך דאָ?

Exercise 8.6

1. לייענען: לייען! לייענט!
2. עסן: עס! עסט!

3. שרײַבן: שרײַב! שרײַבט!
4. זײַן: זײַ! זײַט!

Unit 9

Exercise 9.1

Note: These sentences offer all the possible permutations: they do not necessarily make logical sense.

1. Provided as example
2. איך לייען אָבער/אָדער/אויב/און/אַז/ביז/ווײַל/כאָטש איך עס.
3. מען לייענט אַ בוך אָבער/אָדער/אויב/און/אַז/ביז/ווײַל/כאָטש מען שרײַבט ניט.
4. מיר זײַנען דאָ אָבער/אָדער/אויב/און/אַז/ביז/ווײַל/כאָטש זיי זײַנען ניטאָ.
5. דאָס בוך איז גוט אָבער/אָדער/אויב/און/אַז/ביז/ווײַל/כאָטש איך לייען איצט.

Exercise 9.2

Note: These sentences offer all the possible permutations: they do not necessarily make logical sense.

1. Provided as example.
2. I read/am reading but/or/if/and/until/because/although I eat/am eating.
3. One reads/is reading a book but/or/if/and/until/because/although one does not write/is not writing.
4. We are here but/or/if/and/until/because/although they are not here.
5. The book is good but/or/if/and/until/because/although I am reading now.

Exercise 9.3

1. Provided as example
2. איך לייען, עס איך.
3. מען לייענט אַ בוך, שרײַבט מען ניט.
4. מיר זײַנען דאָ, זײַנען זיי ניטאָ.
5. דאָס בוך איז גוט, לייען איך איצט.

Exercise 9.4

1. Provided as example.
2. I read/am reading so I eat/am eating.
3. One reads/is reading a book so one does not write/is not writing.
4. We are here so they are not here.
5. The book is good so I am reading now.

Unit 10

Exercise 10.1

1. געבן: איך גיב, דו גיסט, ער/זי/עס/מען גיט, מיר גיבן, איר גיט, זיי גיבן; גיב! גיט!
2. האָבן: איך האָב, דו האָסט, ער/זי/עס/מען האָט, מיר האָבן, איר האָט, זיי האָבן; האָב! האָט!
3. וויסן: איך ווייס, דו ווייסט, ער/זי/עס/מען ווייס(ט), מיר ווייסן, איר ווייסט, זיי ווייסן; ווייס! ווייסט!
4. זײַן: איך בין, דו ביסט, ער/זי/עס/מען איז, מיר זײַנען, איר זײַט, זיי זײַנען; זײַ! זײַט!
5. טאָן: איך טו, דו טוסט, ער/זי/עס/מען טוט, מיר טוען, איר טוט, זיי טוען; טו! טוט!

Exercise 10.2

1. עס גיט. third person singular
2. מען טוט. third person singular
3. האָט איר? second person plural
4. די מאַמע ווייס(ט). third person singular
5. דו גיסט. second person singular
6. אַלע מענטשן גיבן. third person plural
7. איך ווייס. first person singular
8. גיב! (second person singular)
9. טוט! (second person plural)
10. האָט! (second person plural)

Exercise 10.3

1. It gives/is giving.
2. One does/is doing.
3. Do you have/are you having?
4. The mother knows.
5. You give/are giving.
6. All people give/are giving.
7. I know.
8. Give!
9. Do!
10. Have!

Unit 11

Exercise 11.1

1. דאָס קליינע בוך nominative
דאָס קליינע בוך neuter, singular, accusative
2. די גוטע מאַמע nominative
די גוטע מאַמע feminine, singular, accusative
3. אַ שיינער מענטש nominative
אַ שיינעם מענטש masculine, singular, accusative
4. גרויסע ביכער nominative
גרויסע ביכער neuter, plural, accusative
5. די פֿריילעכע מענטשן nominative
די פֿריילעכע מענטשן masculine, plural, accusative

Exercise 11.2

1. אונדזערע מאַמעס האָבן שיינע ביכער.

1. Verb: האָבן; third person, plural.
2. Nominative: אונדזערע מאַמעס; feminine, plural.
3. Accusative: שיינע ביכער; neuter, plural.

2. לייענסטו אַ שיין בוך?

1. Verb: לייענסטו; second person, singular.
2. Nominative: דו integrated into the verb; second person, singular.
3. Accusative: אַ שיין בוך; neuter, singular.

3. איך האָב אַ גוטע מאַמע.

1. Verb: האָב; first person, singular.
2. Nominative: איך; first person, singular.
3. Accusative: אַ גוטע מאַמע; feminine, singular.

4. וואָס ווייס(ט) דער מענטש?

1. Verb: ווייס; third person, singular (irregular stem in the present tense).
2. Nominative: דער מענטש; masculine, singular.
3. Accusative: וואָס; interrogative pronoun that does not decline.

5. איך ווער אַ גוטער מענטש.

1. Verb: ווער; first person, singular.
2. Nominative: איך; first person, singular + אַ גוטער מענטש; masculine, singular.
3. Accusative: none.

6. מען האָט דעם מענטש.

1. Verb: האָט; third person, singular.
2. Nominative: מען; third person, singular, impersonal.
3. Accusative: דעם מענטש; masculine, singular.

7. אַלע מענטשן האָבן מאַמעס.

1. Verb: האָבן; third person, plural.
2. Nominative: אַלע מענטשן; masculine, plural.
3. Accusative: מאַמעס; feminine, plural.

8. ביכער האָט ער ניט!

1. Verb: האָט; third person, singular.
2. Nominative: ער; third person, singular.
3. Accusative: ביכער; neuter, plural.

9. איך לייען בערגעלסאָנען.

1. Verb: לייען; first person, singular.
2. Nominative: איך; first person, singular.
3. Accusative: בערגעלסאָנען; masculine, singular (the name of a male author).

10. זי האָט מאָטלען.

1. Verb: האָט; third person, singular.
2. Nominative: זי; third person, singular.
3. Accusative: מאָטלען; masculine, singular (the man's name: Motl).

Exercise 11.3

1. Our mothers have nice books.
2. Are you (singular/informal) reading a nice book?
3. I have a good mother.
4. What does this person know?
5. I am becoming a good person.
6. One has the person./The person is had (i.e. held).
7. All people have mothers.
8. He has no *books*!
9. I am reading Bergelson (the author).
10. She has Motl.

Exercise 11.4

1. איך האָב ניט קיין גוטע ביכער.
2. ווער איז דער גרויסער מענטש?
3. זיי האָבן דאָס קליינע בוך.
4. מיר האָבן אַ גוטן מענטש.
5. זי האָט ניט קיין מאַמע.

Unit 12

Exercise 12.1

1. די מאַמע שרײַבט אַ בוך אויף ייִדיש.
2. די מאַמע שרײַבט אַ בוך וועגן ייִדיש.
3. מיר פֿאָרן אין ניו־יאָרק.
4. מיר פֿאָרן קיין ניו־יאָרק.
5. די מענטשן זײַנען בײַ מאָטלען.
6. די מענטשן זײַנען מיט מאָטלען.
7. דאָס בוך איז פֿאַר מאָטלען.
8. דאָס בוך איז פֿון מאָטלען.

Exercise 12.2

1. The mother writes/is writing a book in Yiddish.
2. The mother writes/is writing a book about Yiddish.

3, 4. We travel/are traveling to New York. (Both prepositions have the same meaning in this usage and are interchangeable.)

5. The people are at Motl's (place).
6. The people are with Motl.
7. The book is for Motl.
8. The book is from Motl.

Exercise 12.3

1. We sleep/are sleeping here.
2. They are in New York and are reading a book from there.
3. Why are you (plural/formal) not going to a (any) wedding?
4. The mother goes/travels/is going/traveling there to Motl/Motl's (place).
5. Where is he going?

Exercise 12.4

1. איך בין אין דער היים מיט מאָטלען.
2. מיר פֿאָרן ניט אין/קיין ניו־יאָרק אויף קיין חתונה.
3. זי פֿאַרט ניט אַהער: זי איז בײַ מאָטלען.
4. דו שרײַבסט/איר שרײַבט אַ בוך פֿאַר מאָטלען.
5. זיי גייען אַהיים.

Unit 13

Exercise 13.1

Dative form	Accusative form	Gender, number	
דעם גרויסן מענטשן	דעם גרויסן מענטשן	masculine, singular	1
אַ גרויסער שטאָט	אַ גרויסע שטאָט	feminine, singular	2
דעם שיינעם בוך	דאָס שיינע בוך	neuter, singular	3
פֿריילעכע מענטשן	פֿריילעכע מענטשן	masculine, plural	4
אַ גוט בוך	אַ גוט בוך	neuter, singular	5
קליינע מאַמעס	קליינע מאַמעס	feminine, plural	6
אַ שיינעם קלאַס	אַ שיינעם קלאַס	masculine, singular	7
דער פֿריילעכער חתונה	די פֿריילעכע חתונה	feminine, singular	8
די גוטע מאַמעס	די גוטע מאַמעס	feminine, plural	9
אַ גוטן מענטשן	אַ גוטן מענטשן	masculine, singular	10

Reminder: The inflection of the words מענטש and מאַמע (taking on the ending of ן) should be considered exceptional. The pattern for most nouns is not to change forms: what changes is the definite article and adjective.

Exercise 13.2

1. מיר שלאָפֿן בײַ דעם = בײַם גוטן מענטשן.
2. איך ווייס וועגן דער שיינער היים.
3. מען עסט מיט דעם = מיטן גרויסן קלאַס.
4. זיי פֿאָרן אויף דער גרויסער חתונה.
5. איר זײַט פֿון דער קליינער שטאָט.

Exercise 13.3

1. We sleep/are sleeping at the good person's (place).
2. I know about the nice home.
3. One eats/is eating with the big class.
4. They travel/are traveling to the big wedding.
5. You (plural/formal) are from the small city.

Exercise 13.4

Verb Nominatives Accusatives *Prepositions* Datives

1. אַלע מענטשן **זײַנען** *אין* דעם גרויסן קלאַס.
2. זיי **לייענען** דאָס גוטע בוך *וועגן* אַ שיינער שטאָט *בײַ* דער מאַמען.
3. עס **איז** מאָטלען גוט *אויף* דער חתונה און די מענטשן **געפֿעלן** דער מאַמען.
4. זי **פֿאָרט** *קיין* ניו-יאָרק *מיט* דער מאַמען.
5. איך **גיב** דעם גוטן מענטשן דער מאַמענס בוך.

Note: דער מאַמענס is possessive but the word בוך remains nominative.

Exercise 13.5

1. All (of the) people are in the big class.
2. They read/are reading the good book about a nice city at the mother's/Mother's (place).
3. Motl is feeling good at the wedding and the mother likes the people.
4. She travels/is traveling to New York with the (her) mother.
5. I give/am giving the good person the mother's book. / I give/am giving the mother's book to the good person.

Unit 14

Exercise 14.1

1. Verb: טוט. Third person singular.

   Noun phrase: די מאַמע. Feminine, singular, nominative (its form indicates that it is nominative or accusative; it agrees with the verb and complies with S-V-O word order).

   {עס} This pronoun is third person, singular. It will be in the accusative case: טוט + *what/whom*? The declined pronoun form is:

   די מאַמע טוט **עס**.

2. Verb: גיט. Third person singular.

   Noun phrase 1: דער מענטש. Masculine, singular, nominative (its form indicates that it can only be nominative).

   Noun phrase 2: דאָס בוך. Neuter, singular, accusative (its form indicates that it is nominative or accusative but we already have a subject for the verb, דער מענטש).

   {ווער} This pronoun will be in the dative case: give + *to what/to whom*? The declined pronoun form is:

   וועמען גיט דער מענטש דאָס בוך?

3. Verb: פּאָרט. Third person singular or second person plural.
   Noun phrase: דער שיינער שטאָט. Feminine, singular, dative (it follows a preposition: אין).
   {מען} Third person singular impersonal. This pronoun is impersonal: it only exists in the nominative case. It must therefore be the subject of the verb.

   מען פּאָרט אין דער שיינער שטאָט.

4. Verb: גיי. First person singular.
   Pronoun: איך. First person, singular, nominative.
   {איר} This pronoun is second person, plural. It will be in the dative case: it follows the preposition: מיט. The declined pronoun form is: איך גיי מיט **אײַך**.

5. Verb: געפֿעלט. Third person singular or second person plural.
   Noun phrase: דאָס בוך. Neuter, singular, nominative: it is the subject of the verb.
   {מיר} This pronoun is first person, plural. It will be in the dative case because this verb requires the dative case. The declined pronoun form is:

   דאָס בוך געפֿעלט **אונדז** ניט.

Exercise 14.2

1. The mother is doing it.
2. Whom is the person giving the book?/The person is giving the book to whom?
3. One travels/is traveling to the nice/attractive city./The attractive city is being traveled to.
4. I go/am going with you (plural or formal).
5. We do not like the book.

Exercise 14.3

1. **זי** עסט.
2. איך ווייס ניט ווער **ער** איז.

Note: Here ווער is a relative pronoun, which acts as a conjunction that links the two phrases together.

3. **זיי** האָבן זיי.
4. אַלע מענטשן גייען מיט **איר**.
5. ווער לייענט **עס**?

Exercise 14.4

1. She eats/is eating.
2. I do not know who he is.
3. They have them.
4. All (of the) people go/are going with her.
5. Who reads/is reading it?

Exercise 14.5

1. ער ווייס(ט) עס זייער גוט.
2. פֿאַרוואָס גיט זי אים יעדער בוך?
3. איך טו עס ניט!
4. ווער איז זייער מאַמע?
5. קיינער פֿאָרט ניט מיט איַיך.

Unit 15

Exercise 15.1

1. The people play/are playing.
2. He gives/is giving himself a good book.
3. Study (plural/formal) Yiddish!
4. The people give/are giving each other nice books.
5. Why is one not studying?

Unit 16

Exercise 16.1

The person likes/loves the book.	1. דער מענטש האָט ליב דאָס בוך.
He (can also be she) likes/loves it.	2. ער האָט עס ליב.
We like/love the mother.	3. מיר האָבן ליב די מאַמע.
We like/love her.	4. מיר האָבן זי ליב.
Whom do you like/love?	5. וועמען האָט איר ליב?

Exercise 16.2

The person does not like/love the book.	1. דער מענטש האָט ניט ליב דאָס בוך.
He (can also be she) does not like/love it.	2. ער האָט עס ניט ליב.
We do not like/love the mother.	3. מיר האָבן ניט ליב די מאַמע.

We do not like/love her. — 4. מיר האָבן זי ניט ליב.
Whom do you not like/love? — 5. ווועמען האָט איר ניט ליב?

Exercise 16.3

1. זי האָט ניט ליב צו שלאָפֿן.
2. מיר האָבן ליב צו עסן.
3. זיי האָבן ליב צו לייענען אין פּאַרק.
4. איך האָב ליב צו זײַן דאָ.
5. האָבן אַלע מענטשן ליב צו לייענען?

Exercise 16.4

1. *We love her!*
   Nominative: we (first person plural): מיר
   Verb: love (first person plural): האָבן ליב
   Accusative: her (first person singular): זי
   Yiddish: מיר האָבן זי ליב.

2. *People like to play with us.*
   Nominative: people (third person plural): מענטשן
   Verb: like (third person plural): האָבן ליב
   to play (infinitive): שפּילן
   Dative (because of preposition, "with"): us (first person plural): אונדז
   Yiddish: משנטשן האָבן ליב צו שפּילן מיט אינדז.

3. *Give (plural) me the book!*
   Nominative: NA (embedded in verb: second person plural)
   Verb: give (second person plural/formal): גיט
   Dative (indirect object, implied "to"): me (first person singular): מיר
   Yiddish: גיט מיר דאָס בוך!

4. *I am not reading it (the book).*
   Nominative: I (first person singular): איך
   Verb: reading (first person plural): לייען
   Accusative: it (third person singular, neuter): עס
   Yiddish: איך לייען עס ניט.

5. *Who is writing them (the books) in Yiddish?*
   Nominative: who (interrogative pronoun): ווער
   Verb: is writing (third person singular): שרײַבט
   Dative 1 (indirect object, implied "to"): them (third person plural): זיי
   Dative 2 (following a preposition): Yiddish: ייִדיש
   Yiddish: ווער שרײַבט זיי אויף ייִדיש?

Unit 17

Exercise 17.1

1. איך זאָל גיין אַהיים איצט.
2. מען מוז עסן גוט.
3. דו טאָרסט ניט שפּילן זיך דאָ.
4. אַלע מענטשן דאַרפֿן שלאָפֿן.
5. די מאַמע זאָל זיך לערנען.
6. איר מעגט שרייַבן.
7. זיי קענען לייענען.

Exercise 17.2

1. I should go home now.
2. One must eat well.
3. You (singular/informal) may not/are not permitted to play here.
4. All people need/have to sleep.
5. The mother should/ought to study.
6. You (plural/informal) may write.
7. They can/are able to read.

Exercise 17.3

1. I want you to eat a little.
2. Let him study!
3. A person must know Yiddish.
4. I do not want your (plural/informal) book.
5. Let me sleep!

Exercise 17.4

1. לאָמיך עסן איצט!
2. זי וויל, איך זאָל לייענען דאָס בוך. / זי וויל אַז איך זאָל לייענען דאָס בוך.
3. איך וויל עס ניט לייענען.
4. זאָלן זיי פֿאָרן אין דער גרויסער שטאָט!
5. מען ווייס(ט) אַז מען דאַרף עסן און שלאָפֿן.

Unit 18

Exercise 18.1

1. דו וועסט שלאָפֿן
2. די מענשטן וועלן לייענען

3. זי וועט האָבן
4. איך וועל טאָן
5. מען וועט געבן
6. מיר וועלן זײַן
7. וועט איר עסן?

Exercise 18.2

1. זיי **וועלן גיין** אין קלאַס.
2. ווער **וועט עסן** בײַ אונדז?
3. מען **וועט געבן** דער מאַמען אַ בוך.
4. איך **וועל** עס ניט **טאָן**.
5. דו **וועסט וועלן שרײַבן**.

Exercise 18.3

1. They go/are going to class./They will go/be going to class.
2. Who eats/is eating at our place?/Who will eat/be eating at our place?
3. One gives/is giving the mother a book./One will give/will be giving the mother a book./The mother is given a book./The mother will be given a book.
4. I do not do/am not doing it./I shall not do/be doing it.
5. You want to write./You will want to write.

Unit 19

Exercise 19.1

1. האָבן: האָבן + געהאַט
איך האָב געהאַט, דו האָסט געהאַט, ער/זי/עס/מען האָט געהאַט, מיר האָבן געהאַט, איר האָט געהאַט, זיי האָבן געהאַט

2. *לייענען: האָבן + געלייענט
איך האָב געלייענט, דו האָסט געלייענט, ער/זי/עס/מען האָט געלייענט, מיר האָבן געלייענט, איר האָט געלייענט, זיי האָבן געלייענט

3. זײַן: זײַן + געווען
איך בין געווען, דו ביסט געווען, ער/זי/עס/מען איז געווען, מיר זײַנען געווען, איר זײַט געווען, זיי זײַנען געווען

4. טאָן: האָבן + געטאָן
איך האָב געטאָן, דו האָסט געטאָן, ער/זי/עס/מען האָט געטאָן, מיר האָבן געטאָן, איר האָט געטאָן, זיי האָבן געטאָן

5. געבן: האָבן + געגעבן
איך האָב געגעבן, דו האָסט געגעבן, ער/זי/עס/מען האָט געגעבן,
מיר האָבן געגעבן, איר האָט געגעבן, זיי האָבן געגעבן

6. גיין: זײַן + געגאַנגען
איך בין געגאַנגען, דו ביסט געגאַנגען, ער/זי/עס/מען איז געגאַנגען,
מיר זײַנען געגאַנגען, איר זײַט געגאַנגען, זיי זײַנען געגאַנגען

7. *לערנען: האָבן + געלערנט
איך האָב געלערנט, דו האָסט געלערנט, ער/זי/עס/מען האָט געלערנט,
מיר האָבן געלערנט, איר האָט געלערנט, זיי האָבן געלערנט

8. פֿאָרן: זײַן + געפֿאָרן
איך בין געפֿאָרן, דו ביסט געפֿאָרן, ער/זי/עס/מען איז געפֿאָרן,
מיר זײַנען געפֿאָרן, איר זײַט געפֿאָרן, זיי זײַנען געפֿאָרן

9. *שפילן: האָבן + געשפילט
איך האָב געשפילט, דו האָסט געשפילט, ער/זי/עס/מען האָט געשפילט,
מיר האָבן געשפילט, איר האָט געשפילט, זיי האָבן געשפילט

10. *קענען: האָבן + געקענט
איך האָב געקענט, דו האָסט געקענט, ער/זי/עס/מען האָט געקענט,
מיר האָבן געקענט, איר האָט געקענט, זיי האָבן געקענט

Exercise 19.2

1. אַלע מענטשן האָבן געוואָלט דאָס בוך.
All of the people/everyone wanted the book.

2. זיי האָבן געשפילט מיט אונדז.
They played/were playing with us.

3. מען האָט געגעסן אַ ביסל.
One ate/was eating a little./A little was/was being eaten.

4. ווער האָט זיך געלערנט דאָ?
Who studied/was studying here?

5. די מאַמע איז געווען פֿריילעך.
The mother was happy.

Exercise 19.3

1. זיי **זײַנען געגאַנגען** אין קלאַס.
2. ווער **האָט געגעסן** בײַ אונדז?
3. מען **האָט געגעבן** דער מאַמען אַ בוך.
4. איך **האָב** עס ניט **געטאָן**.
5. דו **האָסט געוואָלט שרײַבן**.

Exercise 19.4

1. זי האָט טאַקע געוואָלט ווערן אַ פֿריילעכער מענטש.
2. מיר האָבן ניט ליב געהאַט זײַן בוך, האָבן מיר עס ניט געלייענט.
3. איך האָב אײַך געגעבן מײַן בוך, טאָ לייענט עס!
4. וועמענס מאַמע איז געגאַנגען אויף דער חתונה אין דער גרויסער שטאָט?
5. מיר האָבן געגעסן זייער גוט און געשלאָפֿן אַ ביסל.

Unit 20

Exercise 20.1

Tense	אויפֿשטיין	פֿאַרשטיין
Present tense	איך שטיי אויף, דו שטייסט אויף, ער/זי/עס/מען שטייט אויף, מיר שטייען אויף, איר שטייט אויף, זיי שטייען אויף	איך פֿאַרשטיי, דו פֿאַרשטייסט, ער/זי/עס/מען פֿאַרשטייט, מיר פֿאַרשטייען, איר פֿאַרשטייט, זיי פֿאַרשטייען
Future tense	איך וועל אויפֿשטיין, דו וועסט אויפֿשטיין, ער/זי/עס/מען וועט אויפֿשטיין, מיר וועלן אויפֿשטיין, איר וועט אויפֿשטיין, זיי וועלן אויפֿשטיין	איך וועל פֿאַרשטיין, דו וועסט פֿאַרשטיין, ער/זי/עס/מען וועט פֿאַרשטיין, מיר וועלן פֿאַרשטיין, איר וועט פֿאַרשטיין, זיי וועלן פֿאַרשטיין
Past tense	איך בין אויפֿגעשטאַנען, די ביסט אויפֿגעשטאַנען, ער/זי/עס/מען איז אויפֿגעשטאַנען, מיר זײַנען אויפֿגעשטאַנען, איר זײַט אויפֿגעשטאַנען, זיי זײַנען אויפֿגעשטאַנען	איך האָב פֿאַרשטאַנען, דו האָסט פֿאַרשטאַנען, ער/זי/עס/מען האָט פֿאַרשטאַנען, מיר האָבן פֿאַרשטאַנען, איר האָט פֿאַרשטאַנען, זיי האָבן פֿאַרשטאַנען

Exercise 20.2

1. ווי וועט זי פֿאַרשטיין וואָס ער טוט?

How will she understand what he does/is doing?

2. ער איז אויפֿגעשטאַנען אָבער ער האָט ניט געוואָלט גיין.

He got up but he did not want to go/walk.

3. מען וועט אָנהייבן צו לייענען אַ בוך איצט.

One will start to read a book now./A book will begun to be read now.

4. ווער פֿאַרשטייט ייִדיש דאָ?

Who understands Yiddish here?

5. די גוטע מענטשן האָבן אָנגעהויבן דאָס בוך.

The good people started/were starting the book.

Exercise 20.3

1. I understand why they do not get up/stand up/are not getting/standing up.
2. We want you to start eating now!
3. Get up and start going/walking!
4. One will know that he understands nothing./It will be known that he understands nothing.
5. The people understood when they had to go/travel.

Exercise 20.4

1. איך שטיי אויף איצט.
2. פֿאַרשטייסטו מיך ניט?
3. מענטשן הייבן אָן צו וויסן וועגן אונדז.
4. לאָמיר אויפֿשטיין און גיין אין פּאַרק.
5. מען וויל אָנהייבן דאָס בוך.

Unit 21

Exercise 21.1

1. We used to go to the park and play.
2. One started to eat, so I had to eat also.
3. Literally: The person had a quick write. Figuratively: The person wrote something quickly/secretly.
4. They are not about to study.
5. Did you use to read constantly?

Exercise 21.2

1. מײַן מאַמע פֿלעג אונדז לייענען שיינע ביכער.
2. לאָמיר כאַפּן אַ לייען.
3. זיי ווילן, / אַז מיר זאָלן האַלטן אין איין שרײַבן.
4. איך וועל ניט האַלטן אין עסן.
5. מיר פֿלעגן ניט שלאָפֿן.

Unit 22

Exercise 22.1

The mothers would travel/have traveled	1. די מאַמעס וואָלטן געפֿאָרן
One would love/like/have loved/liked	2. מען וואָלט ליב געהאַט
You would be/have been	3. דו וואָלסט געווען
The person would become/would have become	4. דער מענטש וואָלט געוואָרן
You would teach/would have taught	5. איר וואָלט געלערנט

Exercise 22.2

If one were to play, one would not read.	1. אויב מען וואָלט זיך געשפּילט, וואָלט מען ניט געלייענט.
If they had traveled, they would have eaten.	2. אויב זיי וואָלטן געפֿאָרן, וואָלטן זיי געגעסן.
If you become happy, you will be a good person.	3. אויב דו ווערסט פֿריילעך, וועסט דו זײַן אַ גוטער מענטש.
If you had known about us, you would not have liked us.	4. אויב איר וואָלט געוווּסט וועגן אונדז, וואָלט איר אונדז ניט ליב געהאַט.
If the mother would get up, she would study.	5. אויב די מאַמע וואָלט אויפֿגעשטאַנען, וואָלט זי אָנגעהויבן צו לערנען זיך.

Exercise 22.3

1. If I were to understand the book, I would like/love it./If I had understood the book, I would have liked/loved it.
2. If one begins to eat nicely, it will be good.
3. We would not play in the park with them!/We would not have played in the park with them!
4. You would get up if you had to./You would have gotten up if you had had to.
5. Would you go with the/that person?/Would you have gone with that person?

Exercise 22.4

1. איך וואָלט ניט געגאַנגען.
2. אויב איך וואָלט געקענט, וואָלט איך עס געטאָן. / ווען איך קען, וואָלט איך עס געטאָן.
3. מען וואָלט ניט געטאָרט האָבן קיין ביכער.
4. אויב איך לייען, וועל איך זײַן פֿריילעך.
5. מיט וועמען וואָלטן מיר זיך געשפּילט?

Unit 23

Exercise 23.1

1. שלאָפֿנדיק איז ער געגאַנגען אין פאַרק.
2. ווּ איז דאָס געדרוקטע בוך?
3. ווער איז דער שרײַבנדיקע מענטשעלע?
4. גיב מיר דאָס געשריבענע ביכל!
5. די מענטשן גייען עסנדיק.

Exercise 23.2

1. Sleeping, he went to the park./He went to the park while sleeping/asleep.
2. Where is the printed book/the book that has been printed?
3. Who is the person who is writing?
4. Give me the little written book/the written secular book.
5. The people go while eating.

Exercise 23.3

1. וויסנדיק אַז עס איז ניט געווען גוט האָב איך געלייענט דאָס בוך.

Note that the entire clause וויסנדיק אַז עס איז ניט געווען גוט is one sentence unit; האָב is in the second position as the inflected verb.

2. דאָס געלייענטנע בוך איז ניטאָ.
3. מען טאָר ניט שרײַבן גייענדיק. / גייענדיק טאָר מען ניט שרײַבן.
4. די פֿאַרשטייענדיקע מענטשן הייבן אָן צו גיין.
5. מיר ווייסן אַז האָבנדיק איין בוך איז ער פֿריילעך.

Unit 24

Exercise 24.1

1. אַן אַנדער מענטש איז געפֿאָרן.

Verb: איז געפֿאָרן
Subject: מענטש (indefinite)

2. מען גיט אונדז דעם אַנדערן שרײַבער.

Verb: גיב
Subject: מען
Direct object: שרײַבער: masculine, singular, accusative
Indirect object: אונדז

3. ווער איז אין דער אַנדערער שטאָט?

Verb: איז
Subject: ווער
Preposition: אין; שטאָט feminine, singular, dative

4. זיי שרײַבן וועגן די אַנדערע מענטשן.

Verb: שרײַבן
Subject: זיי
Preposition: וועגן; מענטשן masculine, plural, dative

5. מיר ווילן אַנדערע ביכער!

Verb: ווילן
Subject: מיר
Direct object: ביכער: neuter, plural, accusative

Exercise 24.2

1. יענער מענטש איז געפֿאָרן.

1. That person traveled.

2. מען גיט אונדז יענע ביכער.

2. One gives/is giving us those books./Those books are being given to us.

3. ווער איז אין יענער שטאָט?

3. Who is in that city?

4. זיי שרײַבן וועגן יענע מענטשן.

4. They write/are writing about those people.

5. מיר ווילן יענע ביכער!

5. We want those books!

Exercise 24.3

1. די מאַמע לייענט דאָס אַנדערע בוך.
2. מען וויל ניט פֿאָרן אין אָט דער דאָזיקער שטעט.
3. מען וויל אַן אַנדערע!
4. יענער איז דער גרויסער שרײַבער.
5. ווו איז יענעמס בוך?

Unit 25

Exercise 25.1

Comparative	Sentence	
דו האָסט אַ שענערע מאַמע.	דו האָסט אַ שיינע מאַמע.	.1
מען שרײַבט וועגן בעסערע ביכער.	מען שרײַבט וועגן גוטע ביכער.	.2
ער לייענט אַ גרעסערן שרײַבער.	ער לייענט אַ גרויסן שרײַבער.	.3
ווער איז בעסער?	ווער איז גוט?	.4
די קלענערע ביכער זײַנען דאָ.	די קליינע ביכער זײַנען דאָ.	.5

Exercise 25.2

Superlative	Sentence	
דו האָסט די שענסטע מאַמע.	דו האָסט אַ שיינע מאַמע.	.1
מען שרײַבט וועגן די בעסטע ביכער.	מען שרײַבט וועגן גוטע ביכער.	.2
ער לייענט דעם גרעסטן שרײַבער.	ער לייענט אַ גרויסן שרײַבער.	.3
ווער איז דער בעסטער?	ווער איז גוט?	.4
די קלענסטע ביכער זײַנען דאָ.	די קליינע ביכער זײַנען דאָ.	.5

Exercise 25.3

1. That person is a little hungrier than me.
2. I am writing *the best book*!
3. Is he nicer/more attractive than her?
4. One is traveling to a better city.
5. He is the greatest writer.

INDEX